Nihongo Notes

日本語ノート

Language and Culture
ことばと文化

Vol. 1

Osamu Mizutani & Nobuko Mizutani
水谷 修・水谷 信子

The Japan Times

First edition: February 2011

English proofreading: Janet Ashby and Jon McGovern
Layout design: Asahi Media International Inc.
Jacket design: Akio Udagawa
Printing: Nikkei Printing Inc.

Published by The Japan Times, Ltd.
5-4, Shibaura 4-chome, Minato-ku, Tokyo 108-0023, Japan
Phone: 03-3453-2013
http://bookclub.japantimes.co.jp/

ISBN978-4-7890-1424-3

Printed in Japan

PREFACE

The first in the "Nihongo Notes" series was published in *The Japan Times*, an English-language newspaper with a long history in Japan, on September 19, 1976. The editors wanted to arouse interest in the Japanese language among readers before the scheduled publication the following year, of *An Introduction to Modern Japanese,* on which the authors were then working. The weekly column was meant to introduce various aspects of Japanese to readers in an easy-to-read essay. We therefore decided on a style of answering foreigners' questions about situations that they encountered everyday while living in Japan.

In the first essay, *"Dochira-e"* (lit., Where are you going?), we discussed a common greeting which expresses concern in one's neighbor's health and welfare but is often misunderstood by foreigners as nosy prying. It started out "One beautiful Sunday morning," reflecting the fact that the column appeared on Sundays, and tells the experience of a Mr. Ernest Lerner, hearing this greeting used. This particular essay is not included in this edition, however, since the greeting itself has ceased to be used in many areas along with urbanization and the weakening of communities. The name Ernest Lerner, with the same pronunciation as that of "earnest learner," luckily attracted many readers, who told us that he reminded them of their own experiences.

The desire of the editors to arouse the interest of readers proved to be successful. "Nihongo Notes" enjoyed a longevity far beyond its intended six-month span, and reached 350 columns in April 1983; it was awarded the International Publication Prize in 1986. The column is still alive as

"Communication Cues." *An Introduction to Modern Japanese* has also proved to be long-lived, achieving its 73th printing in 2009.

However, what we discussed in the 350 "Nihongo Notes" columns has not received sufficient understanding or response, although now bookstores are filled with an enormous number of writings on the Japanese language. More attention and analysis should be paid to what lies behind daily expressions and common phrases, namely, attitudes toward human relationships and social life. The importance of this has long been felt by the authors while working in the field of teaching Japanese as a foreign language. We are very happy to see 100 pieces out of the 350 now published again, thanks to the editor's judicious selection, enabling us to reach a new generation of readers.

January 2011
Osamu and Nobuko Mizutani

Dochira-e? どちらへ
(Where are you going?)

One beautiful Sunday morning, Mr. Earnest Lerner thought he would take a walk. Just as he was leaving his house, he met the old Japanese woman who lived across the road. He immediately said *Ohayoo-gozaimasu* (Good morning) and was trying to think of other expressions he had learned when the woman suddenly asked:

Dochira-e? どちらへ
(Where are you going?)

Mr. Lerner was appalled. What business of hers was it where he was going? He started wondering what the Japanese equivalent of "Mind your own business" was.

Then a young man living in the neighborhood happened to pass by. He also exchanged greetings with the old woman, but when she asked him the same question he replied without hesitation:

Ee, chotto soko-made. ええ、ちょっとそこまで
(Oh, just down the street.)

Upon hearing this exchange Mr. Lerner suddenly realized that he needn't have been specific in answering the woman's question. From then on he followed the young man's example when greeting the woman.

* * *

When a Japanese asks "Dochira-e?" he is not trying to be nosey. The feeling behind this greeting is that the speaker is happy that you are healthy and well-off enough to go out and have a good time, or he is worried that you have to be so busy as to go out.

In any case, this question simply shows that he is concerned about your well-being, and Japanese use it in the same way that English-speaking people never fail to ask "How are you?" whenever they meet someone they know.

"Dochira-e?" (August 1, 1976)

Akemashite omedetoo-gozaimasu
(Happy New Year!)

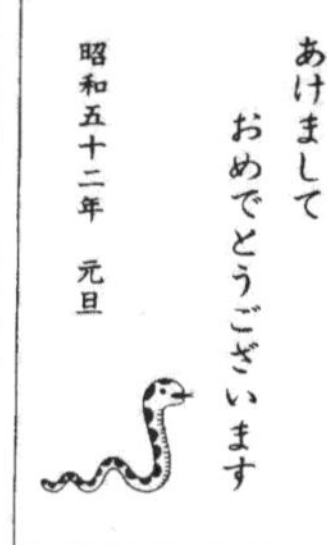

On New Year's Day Mr. Lerner found dozens of greeting cards in his mailbox. Some of them had greetings in *kanji* and some in *hiragana;* some had a picture of a snake, the zodiac symbol for 1977. It was a very pleasant experience to see so many cards together, but he also wondered why they had all come on the same day. He remembered that he had not received a single New Year's card in December, while in the United States Christmas cards start coming early in December and gradually accumulate towards Christmas day.

* * *

New Year's cards mailed before a certain day in December (last month it was Dec. 20) will be delivered on New Year's Day. If you mail your cards later, they will be delivered any day either before or after New Year's Day, just as regular mail is. Japanese try to mail their New Year's cards so that they can be delivered exactly on the Day because it is unseemly for them to arrive before the Day. This seems to be connected with the fact that the Japanese never exchange New Year's greetings before January the first.

New Year's greetings start with the New Year and usually continue to be exchanged for about two weeks.

The most common greetings corresponding to "Happy New Year" are the following two:

Shinnen omedetoo-gozaimasu. (*lit.* We are happy to have the New Year.)

Akemashite omedetoo-gozaimasu. (*lit.* We are happy that New Year's Day has dawned.)

And they are usually followed by

Sakunen-chuu-wa iroiro osewasama-ni narimashita.

Honnen-mo doozo yoroshiku onegai-itashimasu.

These two sentences mean "Thank you very much for everything you did for me last year. Please continue to be kind to me."

We would now like to say to you,

Honnen-Mo doozo yoroshiku onegai-itashimasu.

本年も　どうぞ　よろしく　おねがいいたします。

"Akemashite omedetoo-gozaimasu"
(January 3, 1977)

はしがき

　歴史ある英字新聞 The Japan Times の column に "Nihongo Notes" の最初の記事が掲載されたのは、1976年9月19日であった。著者が執筆を進めていた日本語の教科書『An Introduction to Modern Japanese』が、翌1977年に出版されることになり、その前に英字新聞の読者に日本語への関心と興味を呼び起こしたいという編集部の意向で、日刊新聞の紙面に週1回の column 記事を掲載することになったのである。記事は一般の英字新聞読者を対象に、日本語の諸相を読みやすく伝えるという目的のものであったから、実際の場面で外国人が経験した疑問を提示し、その疑問に答えるという形をとった。

　1976年の最初の記事 *Dochira-e?* は、隣人に対する関心の表現として使われる挨拶が、文字通りの詮索ととられ誤解されるという現象をとりあげたものである。記事が日曜日に掲載されたことを反映して One beautiful Sunday morning で始まり、Mr. Ernest Lerner という英語話者の男性の経験が語られる。この挨拶自体は、都会化が進んで地域の人間関係が希薄になった現在はあまり聞かれなくなったということで、今回の選にもれたが、経験者として登場する Mr. Ernest Lerner の名は earnest learner（熱心な学習者）と発音を同じくするもので、掲載後、何人かの読者から「わたしも Mr. Ernest Lerner だ」という好意ある感想が寄せられた。編集者のもくろみが当たって "Nihongo Notes" は多くの読者の興味を引き、最初6か月の予定であった掲載が延長され1983年4月に350編を数え、1986年に国際出版文化賞を得た。同じ column は現在 "Communication Cues" として続いている。また "Nihongo Notes" が前触れとなった『An Introduction to Modern Japanese』は版を重ね、第73刷を出している。

　しかし、日本語についての評論や解説書が巷にあふれる現在でも、"Nihongo

Notes" 350編に盛られた日本語の諸相についての指摘は、必ずしも十分な理解と反応を得ていない。日本語の表現にみる対人関係意識の検討や、日常の挨拶などの社会言語学的な解釈を論じるものがもっとあるべきではないかと、多年日本語教育に従事した筆者としては痛感してきた。今回、幸いにして編集者の賢明な判断を得て、これまでに出版された "Nihongo Notes 1 ～ 5" 350編から第1巻として50、第2巻として50の計100編が再版される運びになり、もう一度読者の理解を呼びかける機会を得たことは意義深いことで、著者としては喜びに耐えない。

　2巻のうち、第1巻は「文化」編として日常生活で使われる挨拶や表現にひそむ社会的・文化的な意義を中心とし、第2巻は語句の陰影と待遇表現などを主としている。どちらにしても、この中の論議から、語句の詮索を超えて、日本語を使う日本人の心に思いを致すことによって日本語と日本人社会に対する理解を深め、ひいてはその理解を今後の国際社会に生きる上で生かしていただければ、著者としてはまことに幸いである。

2011年1月　水谷修・水谷信子

Index　もくじ

Chapter 3: Consideration toward Others
相手に対する配慮

●本書は『Nihongo Notes 1～5』(ジャパンタイムズ刊) および、その日本語訳版である『外国人の疑問に答える日本語ノート1～4』(同) から「ことばと文化」に関する50編を選び、再編集したものです。

Chapter 1

Daily Language

くらしの中のことば

In this chapter we explain expressions that are used very often in daily life yet are rather difficult for foreigners to understand.

Doomo, originally used in a negative meaning, now actually is used in expressions corresponding to "Thank you very much," "I am very sorry," and even "Hello" or "Good-bye." *Hajimemashite*, an expression used when meeting someone for the first time, should be uttered at an appropriate distance from the listener. The fact that *Konnichiwa*, usually regarded as a greeting corresponding to "Good day," is actually not used towards one's family members is something of which the Japanese themselves are usually unaware.

Aizuchi, response words inserted frequently whenever the speaker pauses, show how the Japanese listener tries to build up the flow of conversation by encouraging and cooperating with the speaker. Japanese refer to the previous meeting with *Senjitsu-wa gochisoosama-deshita* to confirm a good relationship continuing from the past; they express gratitude for the favor done for a family member, with whom the speaker identifies himself. Such expressions offer the reader valuable clues in understanding Japanese society. Also, seeing that *anata*, unlike the English "you," is used to refer to limited persons or how *san*, a common term of respect, is actually used, will provide even the Japanese themselves with an opportunity to think about Japanese society.

　この章の中には、日常の生活の中でよく使われるが、日本に住む外国人にとって理解のむずかしいと思われるもの、言外の意味の知られていないものをとりあげて説明を加えた。

　「どうも」は本来「どうもよくない」のように否定的に意味をもつものであるが、「どうもありがとう」「どうもすみません」、さらに出会いや別れの場面でも使われることや、初対面のあいさつの「はじめまして」を口にする時は相手とどのような間隔を取るべきかについて言及する。ごくあたりまえの出会いの挨拶として考えられがちな「こんにちは」は、実は家族の間では使われないものであって、「こんにちは、おかあさん」など通常は口にしないものであるという、意外に注目されていない事実をも示す。

　日本人が相手の話を聞く時に頻繁にさしいれる相づちは、話し手と聞き手が協力して会話をつくりあげるという意識の強い表れであること、前回の出会いに言及する「先日はごちそうさまでした」、自身と家族を一体化し、家族に対する相手の配慮に感謝する「主人がお世話になっております」など、一見、外国人に理解しがたいような表現を考えることも、日本の社会と日本人の言語生活を知るための貴重ないとぐちを提供するものである。また、「あなた」という代名詞が英語のyouと等価でなく、相手や状況によって使えないこと、「〜さん」という敬称のもつ広がりなど、日本人自身が平常意識していない面についての指摘に注目することで、ことばと生活についての興味深い考察ができよう。

Doomo
どうも
Indeed

One word that bothers Mr. Ernest Lerner now is *doomo*. English-Japanese dictionaries give "indeed" and "somehow" as definitions for it, but he suspects that its actual usage covers a much wider range.

The people at his office, for instance, use *doomo* for many other purposes. They say *Kinoo-wa, doomo* (lit., Indeed yesterday) when they meet; they say just *Doomo* to thank others and to apologize. They also say *Ja, doomo* when they part.

Doomo is used to cut answers short, too. When Mr. Lerner asked Mr. Takada how his study of English was going, he said *Doomo-nee*. He did not mean that his English had made great progress; he meant just the opposite.

*　　　*　　　*

Probably most Japanese do not realize how often they use, or overuse, this word. *Doomo* literally means "in all ways," or "no matter how I look at it." Actually it is used to mean various things. There are two very common uses of *doomo*—as a social expression and as an indication of negative judgment.

As a social expression it is used by itself to mean "Thank you," "Sorry," "Excuse me,"" Thank you for coming," and "Sorry to take your time," to mention just a few. The last two are equivalent to "Hello" and "Good-bye" respectively. In these expressions the part that follows *doomo* is left out;

どうも

Indeed

Mr. Lerner には「どうも」という語がとらえがたい。英和辞典を見ると、"indeed" とか "somehow" と出ているが、実際の用法はもっと広いようである。

たとえば会社の人たちもさまざまな意味で使う。人に会うと「きのうはどうも」と言う。お礼を言う時もあやまる時も「どうも」、そして別れる時は「じゃ、どうも」と言う。

答えを短くする時にも「どうも」を使う。Mr. Takada に、英語の勉強の進歩ぶりをたずねたら、「どうもねえ」と言っていた。これは英語が大いに上達したというのではなく、全然だめの意味であった……。

＊　　　　　＊　　　　　＊

おそらく大抵の日本人は、自分がどれほどこの語を使っているか、いや乱用しているか、気がついていないであろう。文字通りには、"in all ways"（どのようにも）あるいは "no matter how I look at it"（どう考えても）の意味であるが、実際の用法は多様である。特に一般的な 2 つの用法は、社交上の用法と否定的な判断の表明である。

社交上の用法としては、「どうも」単独で、"Thank you," "Sorry," "Excuse me," "Thank you for coming," "Sorry to take your time" など、さまざまな意味に用いられる。最後にあげた 2 つは "Hello" と "Good-bye" に当たる。こうした用法では、「どうも」のあとに来る部分は省略されている。たとえば「どうもありがとうございます」の「ありがとうございます」は言わなくてもわかる。

for example in the case of *Doomo arigatoo-gozaimasu*, *arigatoo-gozaimasu* is understood.

The second usage is also very common. If you ask someone a question and he just says *Watashi-wa doomo . . .* (lit., I somehow . . .) in a hesitant tone, he means that he does not know the answer. Or if you ask someone's opinion about something and the reply is *Doomo . . .* or *Doomo-nee*, it means that he feels negatively about it; Mr. Takada used *doomo* in this way when Mr. Lerner asked him about his study of English.

Doomo changes its meaning depending not only on the situation but also on the tone in which it is spoken. If you pronounce it quickly, it sounds casual. (Some people say *Doomo, doomo* quickly in greeting people; this sounds very casual and cannot be used when you want to be polite or formal.) But if you pronounce it slowly, it sounds sincere and polite. In stating negative judgment, it is pronounced in a hesitant, dangling tone.

(September 19, 1976)

Hajimemashite
はじめまして
How do you do?

The other day Mr. Lerner introduced one of his friends, Miss Winters, to Mr. Takada. When Mr. Lerner and Miss Winters arrived at the lobby of the hotel where they had arranged to meet, Mr. Takada was already there sitting on a sofa. He stood up when he saw them, and they walked over to

第2の用法も一般的である。何か質問された人がためらいがちに「わたしはどうも……」と言ったとすれば、よくわからないの意である。また、意見を求められた人が「どうも……」あるいは「どうもねえ」と答えたとすれば、否定的な感情を抱いているという意味で、Mr. Lerner に英語の進歩ぶりをたずねられた Mr. Takada が使ったのはこの用法である。

「どうも」の意味合いは、その場の状況だけでなく、口調によっても変わる。早口で言えば軽い感じになる。（人に会った時「どうもどうも」と早口で言う人もあるが、これは気楽な調子に聞こえ、丁重な改まった話では使えない。）逆にゆっくり「どうも」と言うと、心のこもった丁重な印象を与える。否定的な判断を表明する時は、ためらいがちな口調で言う。

(1976.9.19)

はじめまして

How do you do?

先日 Mr. Lerner は友人のひとり Miss Winters を Mr. Takada に紹介した。Mr. Lerner と Miss Winters が待ち合わせ場所のホテルのロビーに着くと、Mr. Takada はすでに来てソファに腰をおろしていた。2人を見て彼は立ちあがり、2人はそちらへ歩み寄った。Mr. Lerner が彼を紹介すると、Miss Winters は彼

him. When Mr. Lerner introduced him to Miss Winters, she stepped forward to him and said.

Hajimemashite, Takada-san. Winters-desu.
(How do you do, Mr. Takada? My name is Winters.)

just as Mr. Lerner had told her to do.

But a strange thing happened. Mr. Takada suddenly stepped back away from her and then said

Doozo yoroshiku.
(Glad to meet you.)

Miss Winters was not pleased by this. Later she said that she felt hurt at Mr. Takada's stepping back at the moment he saw her. Was she so frightening? Or did she look so unpleasant? No! Mr. Lerner denied her suspicions. In fact, she was a beautiful young woman, tall and well-built. But as someone who knew something about the Japanese, he thought he could understand why Mr. Takada had stepped back.

Japanese usually keep more distance between them when they talk than Americans do, and the distance is even greater when the two are speaking politely. For most Japanese it is embarrassing to stand too close to someone with whom they should talk politely. Mr. Takada, he emphasized, had stepped back not because he was afraid of her, or because he wanted to hurt her, but because he wanted to be perfectly correct.

*   *   *

When Mr. Lerner asked him if he was right, Sensee said he was. And Sensee added that probably the speaker-listener distance will vary depending on whether the two people bow or shake hands. When the two are going to bow to each other, they have to stand relatively far apart; if they are going to shake hands, they have to stand closer together. And among

のほうへ進み出て、Mr. Lerner に教えられた通り、

　　　ハジメマシテ、タカダサン。ウィンターズデス

と言った。

　ところが奇妙なことが起こった。Mr. Takada は突然あとじさりして、それから、

　　　どうぞよろしく

と言ったのである。

　これは Miss Winters にとって快い経験ではなかった。Mr. Takada が彼女を見るなりあとじさりしたことで、非常に感情を傷つけられたと、あとで Mr. Lerner に訴えた。自分はそんなに恐ろしい顔をしているか。見るからに不愉快か。とんでもないと、Mr. Lerner はその疑いを否定した。事実、Miss Winters は背が高く、均整のとれた、美しい若い女性である。しかし、Mr. Lerner は、いくらか日本の事情がわかる人間として、Mr. Takada があとじさりした理由がわかるような気がした。

　日本人は一般にアメリカ人よりも、相手と離れて話をする。その距離は丁寧な話し合いでは一層大きくなる。大抵の日本人は、丁寧に話すべき相手が、あまり近くに立つと、当惑してしまう。Mr. Takada は、Miss Winters の気を悪くさせるどころか、礼儀正しくありたいと思ったため、後ろへさがったのだと強調した……。

*　　　　　*　　　　　*

　Mr. Lerner が以上の意見を述べると、先生はそれでよいと言った。そして、話し手と聞き手の距離は、おじぎをするか握手をするかによって、変わるのだろうと言った。両者が互いにおじぎをするなら、比較的離れて立つ必要があるし、握手するなら近づく必要がある。またおじぎをする場合でも、おじぎの深さによっ

people bowing, too, the distance can vary according to the degree of bow-ing; the deeper the bow, the greater the distance.

Those who teach Japanese to foreigners often feel embarrassed when their students stand closer than they are expected to. This is especially true when the teacher and the student are of different sexes. In the same way, you may have experienced something awkward about shaking hands with a Japanese because he was standing far away from you.

In conversation, all expressions have to be said not only with the right grammar and right pronunciation, but also with the appropriate manner. This "manner" refers not only to body posture but also to the speaker-listener distance.

(March 12, 1978)

Ojigi
おじぎ
Bowing

Mr. Takada introduced one of his acquaintances, a Mr. Yamamoto, to Mr. Lerner the other day. Mr. Lerner gave him his name card and said as usual, *Hajimemashite* (How do you do?). Then Mr. Yamamoto gave him his name card and said while bowing

Hajimete . . .
(lit., for the first time)

but Mr. Lerner could not hear the rest. He wondered if *Hajimete* can be

て、距離が変わってくる。おじぎが深ければ深いほど、距離は遠くなる。

　外国人に日本語を教える教師は、学生が通常期待されるより近く寄ってくるので、当惑することがある。教師と学習者が異性の場合はなおさらである。また、日本人と握手しようとして、相手が遠く離れているのでやりにくかった経験もあると思われる。

　人と話す時、正しい方法と正しい発音とでものを言うだけでなく、適切な態度で話す必要がある。この「態度」の中には、体の動かしかただけでなく、話し手と聞き手との距離も関係してくる。

(1978.3.12)

おじぎ

Bowing

　先日 Mr. Takada が友人の Mr. Yamamoto を紹介してくれたので、Mr. Lerner は名刺を渡し、いつものように「ハジメマシテ」とあいさつした。Mr. Yamamoto も自分の名刺を渡し、おじぎしながら何か言ったが、

　　　はじめて……

の次は聞きとれなかった。「はじめて」は「はじめまして」と同じように使われるのだろうかと Mr. Lerner は思ったが、あとで Mr. Takada にきいてみると、実

used in the same way as *Hajimemashite*. Later Mr. Takada explained that Mr. Yamamoto had actually said

Hajimete ome-ni kakarimasu.

(How do you do? —lit., This is the first time to meet you.)

He realized that *Hajimemashite* is the abbreviation of *Hajimete ome-ni kakarimasu* and also learned that the last half of a sentence can be said in a very low voice that can hardly be heard.

*   *   *

Polite expressions are often said while bowing. When one says a polite expression with a bow, the last part of the expression is usually said in a low voice because it can be understood without being said clearly. In such expressions as *Hajimete ome-ni kakarimasu, doozo yoroshiku onegai-shimasu* (Glad to meet you or, Please do it for me, depending on the situation— lit., Please be good to me) or *Kono tabi-wa makoto-ni arigatoo-gozaimashita* (Thank you very much for what you have done for me), the last part is usually said very softly when said while bowing.

When one expresses politeness by bowing in personal situations, one slowly bends one's whole body forward and downward: sometimes one even bends his knees slightly. A quick bow will give an impression of casualness or insincerity, and an abrupt bow will seem childish; to spend the appropriate time bowing, it will help to say, either audibly or inaudibly, such phrases as *arigatoo-gozaimashita* or *yoroshiku onegai-shimasu* while bending one's body over.

And one should bow at the same time as the other person does. It is embarrassing to straighten up from bowing long before the other person does. In order to bow in accordance with the other person, it is important to observe him as he starts bowing.

(April 26, 1981)

際に Mr. Yamamoto が言ったのは、

　　　はじめてお目にかかります

だったのだそうである。

　なるほど、「はじめまして」は「はじめてお目にかかります」の略なのだなと納得したが、同時に、文の後半は聞こえないほど低い声で言うこともあるのだと思った……。

＊　　　　　　　　＊　　　　　　　　＊

　丁寧なあいさつは、おじぎをしながら言うことが多い。おじぎをしながら言う時、文の後半の部分は低い声で言うのが普通で、これは、はっきり言わなくてもわかるからである。「はじめてお目にかかります。どうぞよろしくお願いします」や、「この度はまことにありがとうございました」などの場合、終わりのほうはおじぎをしながら極めて小さい声で言うのが普通である。

　個人同士のあいさつで、礼儀正しくおじぎする場合は、全身を前の方へゆっくりと時間をかけて曲げる。わずかながら膝まで曲げることもある。時間をかけずにおじぎをすると、気楽な、あるいは気のない印象を与えるし、ぴょこんと頭を下げるのは幼稚に見える。適切な時間を費やしておじぎをするには、体を曲げながら、声を出しても出さなくてもよいから、「ありがとうございました」とか「よろしくお願いします」と言ってみるとよい。

　また、おじぎは、相手と同じ時にしなければならない。こちらが頭をあげてしまったのに相手がなかなか頭をあげないのは、気まずいことである。相手に合わせておじぎをするために、相手がおじぎし始める時よく観察することが大切である。

(1981.4.26)

Konnichiwa
こんにちは
Good afternoon

Mr. Ernest Lerner went to his office late one day. It was almost two in the afternoon so he said, instead of *Ohayoo-gozaimasu* (Good morning),

Konnichiwa.
(Good afternoon.)

There were several people working in the office. All of them turned to him, but they did not say anything for a moment; then some of them said *Konnichiwa* hesitantly; others just nodded silently.

Mr. Lerner did not understand. Why did *Konnichiwa* sound strange? Isn't it a perfectly reasonable greeting, corresponding to English greetings such as "Good morning," "Good day," or "Hello"?

*　　　　*　　　　*

As far as the hour of the day is concerned, it is proper to say *Konnichiwa* at two in the afternoon, but it is not appropriate to say it to one's colleagues.

Among the several greetings exchanged when meeting people, *Ohayoo-gozaimasu* can be used to any person, to people in any relationship with you, but the situations where *Konnichiwa* and *Konbanwa* (Good evening) can be used are rather limited. These two are used with people who do not belong to one's own group.

こんにちは

Good afternoon

　Mr. Lerner はその日会社に遅く出勤した。もう午後2時だったので、「おはようございます」の代わりに、

　　コンニチハ

と言った。

　室内では数人の社員が仕事をしていた。全員 Mr. Lerner のほうを見たが、しばらくは何も言わなかった。やがて何人かが「こんにちは」と言いにくそうに言った。他の人たちは黙って頭をさげた。

　Mr. Lerner にはわからなかった。どうして「こんにちは」ではおかしいのか。英語で "Good morning," "Good day," "Hello" などと言うのと同じ、ちゃんとしたあいさつではないか……。

＊　　　　　＊　　　　　＊

　1日の時間帯という点から言えば、午後2時には「こんにちは」がふさわしいが、同僚に対するあいさつとしては適切ではない。

　人に会った時のあいさつとして、「おはようございます」は誰にでも、どんな間柄の人に対してでも使える。しかし、「こんにちは」と「こんばんは」が使われる場面は限られている。この2つは、自分と同じ集団に属している人には使わない。

Needless to say, they cannot be used among family members. People working at the same office are usually considered to be members of one's own group, though people's conception of the size or content of this group varies according to the individual.

The people at Mr. Lerner's office regarded him as a member of their group; which is why they were embarrassed to be greeted by him with *Konnichiwa*. If they had regarded him as an outsider, they would have accepted it as a matter of fact.

One more thing about *Konnichiwa* and *Konbanwa* is that they do not sound very polite and cannot be used to greet one's superiors. For example, a customer greets a clerk at the store with *Konnichiwa* or *Konbanwa*, but the clerk does not return the same greeting; he usually says *Irasshaimase* (lit., I'm glad you have come).

When Japanese feel *Konnichiwa* or *Konbanwa* to be inappropriate, they turn to various substitutes, among which referring to the climate is a very popular one; they often greet others by saying that it is very cold, or hot, or that it has been raining a great deal.

(August 29, 1976)

　言うまでもなく、家族の間では使わない。同じ会社で働いている人は、通常自分の集団の一員と考えられる。「集団」の幅や内容についての考え方は、人によって一様ではないが。

　Mr. Lerner の会社の人たちは、彼を同じ集団の一員と見ていた。だから、「こんにちは」と言われた時まごついたのである。もし彼らが Mr. Lerner を外部の人間と見なしていたら、「こんにちは」を当然と受け取ったであろう。

　もうひとつ、「こんにちは」と「こんばんは」について注意すべきことは、どちらも丁寧な印象を与えないので、目上の人には使えないということである。お客は店員に「こんにちは」「こんばんは」と言うが、店員のほうは同じことは言わない。通常「いらっしゃいませ」と言う。

　「こんにちは」や「こんばんは」が不適切だと感じられる時には、他のあいさつの方法が考えられるが、その中では天候気候に関するものが多い。寒いとか暑いとか、よく降るというようなことが、あいさつ代わりに言われる。

> ▶英語やドイツ語にも似た傾向はある。Good morning. や Guten Morgen. は家族同士で使うが、Good afternoon. や Guten Tag. は使わないということである。

(1976.8.29)

Raishawaa-san
ライシャワーさん
Mr. Reischauer

Mr. Ernest Lerner likes to use *san*, a Japanese term of respect; it can stand for Mr., Mrs., and Miss, and it can be attached to first names as well as last names. It is less discriminatory than English terms which distinguish male from female, and married woman from unmarried, though recently many women are beginning to prefer Ms.

The other day, when Mr. Lerner referred to Prof. Reischauer, he said

Raishawaa-san.

(Mr. Reischauer.)

Miss Yoshida, one of the listeners at that time, interrupted him and asked if he knew the former ambassador personally. He said no, and wanted to ask her why she had raised that question, but the conversation went on too rapidly and he did not have the chance to do so.

*   *   *

As Mr. Lerner feels, *san* is a very convenient suffix. It is added not only to people's names, but also to the names of occupations such as *omawari-san* (policeman), *yuubin'ya-san* (mailman), *nikuya-san* (butcher), and *un-tenshu-san* (driver).

The Japanese also use *san* in various types of relationships such as *okyaku-san* (customer) and *otonari-san* (people living next door). Why not *Raishawaa-san*?

ライシャワーさん

Mr. Reischauer

Mr. Lerner は日本語の敬称「さん」が気に入っている。Mr.、Mrs.、Miss いずれの代わりにも使えるし、姓だけでなく名のほうにもつく。男性女性を区別し、既婚女性と未婚女性を区別する（最近は Ms. を使う人も増えてきたが）英語に比べて、差別のない敬称である。

先日、ライシャワー教授の話をしていた時、Mr. Lerner が、

ライシャワーサン

と言ったら、話を聞いていた Miss Yoshida がライシャワー大使と知り合いかとたずねた。「いいえ、なぜですか」とたずねたいと思ったが、話がどんどん進んで行って、機を逸してしまった……。

*　　　　　*　　　　　*

Mr. Lerner の感想どおり、「さん」は極めて便利な接尾辞で、人名のみならず職業名にもつく——「おまわりさん」「郵便屋さん」「肉屋さん」「運転手さん」のように。

また、「お客さん」「お隣さん」のように、各種の人間関係を示す語にもつく。なぜ「ライシャワーさん」が不適切なのか。

前駐日大使ならば、当然敬意を表すべき人物であるが、一般に日本語の中では「さん」がつかない。前大使のみならず、有名な政治家や学界の権威なども、個人的な知己でない限り、「さん」づけでは呼ばれない。「さん」は敬意だけでな

The former ambassador to Japan is certainly a person worthy of respect, but he is usually called without *san* in Japanese. Not only he but also great Japanese statesmen and outstanding people in academic fields are deprived of *san*, unless they are personal acquaintances of the speaker. *San* does not show respect only; it also indicates intimacy.

The infamous as well as the famous are also deprived of *san*. The only exception is, if you want to make people laugh, you can say *doroboo-san* (Mr. Thief), or *obake-san* (Mr. Monster).

San has one more peculiarity about which you should be careful. It cannot be used with one's own name or the names of one's family members. In English, people sometimes add Mr., Mrs., or Miss to their own names and say "This is Mr. Jones speaking," or "I'm Mrs. Smith." But in Japanese you have to be very careful not to add *san* to your own name, and particularly not to the name of your wife when referring to her.

(September 5, 1976)

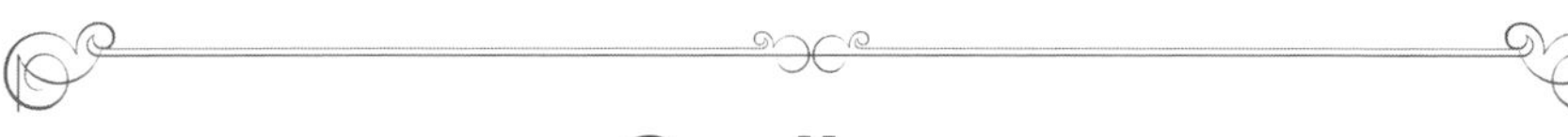

Sonii-san

ソニーさん

Mr. Sony

Miss Winters told Mr. Lerner the other day that she had been working a few months for a trading company called "Suzuki-Booeki." She said that she had had an interesting experience just a couple of days before.

When she answered the phone, the speaker said

く、親近感をも表すのである。

　有名人に「さん」がつかないのと同様、不名誉な人間にも「さん」がつかない。「泥棒さん」「お化けさん」など、人を笑わせる時以外には用いない。

　「さん」についてもうひとつ注意すべきことは、自分自身や家族の名前にはつかないということである。英語では自分の名に Mr.、Mrs.、Miss をつけて、"This is Mr. Jones speaking."（こちらはスミスです）とか "I'm Mrs. Smith." と言ったりする。しかし日本語では、自分や妻の名前に「さん」をつけないよう、注意する必要がある。

(1976.9.5)

ソニーさん

Mr. Sony

　Miss Winters は、数か月前から、鈴木貿易という会社に勤めている。2、3日前そこでおもしろい経験をしたと言って、Mr. Lerner に次のような話をした。

　電話に出ると相手が、

Moshi-moshi, Suzuki-Booeki-san-desu-ka.

She took it as "Hello, Miss Suzuki-Booeki?" and said "No" instantly, and hung up. But just the next moment she heard one of her colleagues saying

Sonii-san-desu-ka. Kochira-wa Suzuki-Booeki-desu.
(Hello, Mr. Sony? This is the Suzuki Trading Company.)

*   *   *

The suffix *san* is added to people's names, both first and last, and to occupations as in *omawari-san* (Mr. Policeman). Not only that, it is used with stores, too; *yaoya-san* means either "a greengrocer" or "a vegetable store." Sometimes names of stores are said with *san*, usually by women, as in

Mikawaya-san-de kaimashita.
(I bought it at Mikawaya.)

In a similar way *san* is added to the name of companies probably because they are personified. Most businessmen refer to other companies with *san* as if they were human beings, as in

Sonii-san-towa torihiki-ga arimasu.
(We deal with Sony.)
Hitachi-san-niwa itsumo osewa-ni natte-orimasu.
(We deal with Hitachi. —lit., Mr. Hitachi is always kind to us.)

It can be said that names of companies are treated like family names; therefore

Sonii-san-wa doo-desu-ka.
(How about you, Mr. Sony?)

　　もしもし、鈴木貿易さんですか

と言ったので、"Miss Suzuki-Booeki?" という意味だと思って、言下に「いいえ」
と言って切ってしまった。次の瞬間、同僚が、

　　ソニーさんですか。こちらは鈴木貿易です

と言っているのを聞いたが、あとの祭だった……。

＊　　　　　＊　　　　　＊

　「さん」という敬称は人名につける。姓にも名にもつける。また職業名にもつ
けて「おまわりさん」のように言う。そればかりでなく、店にもつける。「やお
やさん」は「野菜を売る人」でもあり「野菜を売る店」でもある。
　これは女性に多いが、

　　三河屋さんで買いました

のように言う。
　同時に会社の名前にも「さん」をつける。会社を人間扱いしているわけであろ
う。他の会社には、人名と同じく、

　　ソニーさんとは取引があります

とか、

　　日立さんにはいつもお世話になっております

などと言う。
　この場合は会社名が姓のように扱われるので、ソニーの社員に対しても、

　　ソニーさんはどうですか

is said to someone from Sony. The idea is that the person belongs to a family whose name is Sony.

But it must be noted that *san* is used in this way only when the speaker is engaged in business with the company or the institution. You can say that *san* is used as an endearment rather than a sign of respect. The teller at the bank will call the owner of the passbook (*tsuuchoo*) to the window saying *Sonii-san* or *Kokuritsu Kokugo Kenkyuujo-san* (Mr. National Language Research Institute), because they are the bank's valued customers.

(June 24, 1979)

Aizuchi
あいづち

How Japanese listen

Mr. Ernest Lerner wanted to tell Mrs. Matsumoto, his landlady, about his recent trip. When he finished the first phrase, *Senshuu umi-e ittara* (When I went to the sea last week), Mrs. Matsumoto immediately said,

Ee, ee.

(Yes, yes.)

Mr. Lerner was somewhat surprised by this unexpected response, but tried to continue. He said, *Mizu-wa kiree-datta-n-desu-ga* (the water was clean, but), then again Mrs. Matsumoto said,

Soo-desu-ka.

(Is that so?)

などと話しかける。ソニー家という家族の一員、という考えかたがあるのであろう。

　しかし、「さん」がこのように使われるのは、その会社や機関と取引のある場合だけである。「さん」は尊敬のしるしというよりは、親しみの表現である。銀行の窓口で通帳の持ち主を呼ぶ時にも、大切なお客さまを呼ぶのであるから、「ソニーさん」とか「国立国語研究所さん」（あるいは「〜さま」）と呼ぶ。

(1979.6.24)

相づち

How Japanese listen

　大家さんの Mrs. Matsumoto と話している時、最近の旅行が話題になったが、Mr. Lerner が「先週海へ行ッタラ……」と言いかけると、夫人はすぐ、

　　ええ、ええ

と言った。Mr. Lerner は予期せぬ返事に驚いたが、話を続けた。「水ハキレイダッタンデスガ……」と言うと、また、

　　そうですか

Mr. Lerner almost screamed, *Hito-ga oozee-de* (there were so many people), and Mrs. Matsumoto agreed,

Soo-deshoo-ne.

(It must be so.)

In this way Mrs. Matsumoto kept throwing in short answers until Mr. Lerner felt that his Japanese was so poor that she did not want to listen to him, and he cut the conversation short.

*   *   *

Short answers such as *Hai, Ee, Soo-desu-ka, Soo-deshoo-ne*, which are called *aizuchi* are used as a signal to show that the listener is listening attentively and wants the speaker to go on. Japanese feel uneasy when the listener remains silent without giving *aizuchi*.

Japanese believe, in most cases unconsciously, that the flow of speech is made up not only by the speaker but also by the listener who participates by giving *aizuchi*. Sometimes, the listener goes so far as to finish up what the speaker is going to say. Two people, A and B, for example, join together in making up one flow of speech; this might be illustrated as

This is quite different from the Western notion of what conversation should be like. Westerners consider it good manners to keep silent without interrupting the speaker while he is speaking.

(August 22, 1976)

と口をはさむ。やけになった Mr. Lerner が「人ガ大勢デ……」と声を張りあげると、Mrs. Matsumoto はすぐ、

　　　そうでしょうね

と賛同する。

　こんなに次々と返事をするのは、自分の日本語がへただから、もう聞きたくないということだろうと、Mr. Lerner は早々に話を切りあげてしまった……。

＊　　　　　　＊　　　　　　＊

　話を聞きながらさしはさむ「はい」「ええ」「そうですか」「そうでしょうね」などの相づちは、「熱心に聞いていますから先をどうぞ」という合図のようなものである。聞き手が相づちを打たないと、話し手は不安になってくる。

　日本人の場合、特に意識しないにせよ、話の流れというものは、話し手だけでなく聞き手も一緒になって形作るもの、と感じている。時には聞き手が話の先を言ってしまうことさえある。話し手と聞き手が一体となって話の流れを作っていく様子は、2本の線でなく、1本の線で表したほうが適当である。

―――＿―――＿―――＿―――＿

　欧米人の場合は全く異なり、話し手が話し終わるまで、口をはさまずに沈黙を守るのが礼儀であると考える。

(1976.8.22)

Itadakimasu
いただきます
I'm going to receive your treat. Thank you.

A few days ago Mr. Takada asked Mr. Lerner to have dinner with his family. They had prepared the New Year's dinner, very colorful and very special. Mr. Lerner decided to be as polite as he could. So when Mr. Takada said according to Japanese custom

Nanimo gozaimasen-ga doozo.

(There isn't much but please start eating.)

Mr. Lerner said politely

Itadakimasu.

(Thank you. —lit., I'm going to receive your treat.)

Then everybody else said the same thing and started eating. Mr. Lerner was a little surprised because he had thought that *Itadakimasu* was used by a guest to thank his host.

*   *   *

Most people say *Itadakimasu* before eating and *Gochisoosama* after eating even in their own home. Children are trained at home never to forget to say these phrases, and when they go to kindergarten or elementary school teachers reinforce this training. Some people disregard this custom when they grow up, but others continue to say these phrases even when

いただきます

I'm going to receive your treat. Thank you.

　2、3日前のこと、Mr. Takada が Mr. Lerner を食事に招いてくれた。行ってみるとお正月の色どりの美しい特別のごちそうが用意してあった。せいぜい礼儀正しくしなければ、と Mr. Lerner は思った。そこで Mr. Takada が日本風に、

　　何もございませんがどうぞ

と言った時、Mr. Lerner は礼儀正しく、

　　いただきます

と答えた。

　そのあと家族全員が同じことを言って食べ始めたので、Mr. Lerner はちょっと驚いた。「いただきます」は、客が主人に対して感謝を述べる言葉だと思っていたのだ……。

＊　　　　　＊　　　　　＊

　大抵の人は自宅であっても、食事の前に「いただきます」と言い、食事の後で「ごちそうさま」と言う。子供たちは家庭で、このあいさつを忘れずに言うようにしつけられ、幼稚園や小学校では、さらに先生たちに訓練される。成人するとこの習慣を捨ててしまう人もあるが、ひとりで食事する時にもこのあいさつをする人が多い。

　「いただきます」も「ごちそうさま」も感謝の言葉である。この感謝は、食事

they eat alone.

Both *Itadakimasu* and *Gochisoosama* are expressions of gratitude. This gratitude is directed to everybody and everything that has made the meal possible. Thus they can be used both as an expression of gratitude to the host and as something like saying grace in the West.

When you are asked to start eating by your host, it is proper to say *Ita-dakimasu* before eating. And you should say *Gochisoosama* (lit., It was a real feast), or more politely, *Gochisoosama-deshita*, after eating. Then the host or hostess will say something to deny this praise, such as

Osomatsusama-deshita.

(You're welcome. —lit., It was a poor meal.)

It is not Japanese custom to say "I'm glad you liked it."

Another point about *Gochisoosama* is that it is used as an expression of thanks, not just for food, but also for hospitality. For instance, when leaving a party at someone's home, Americans might say to the host or hostess "Thank you very much. I had a wonderful time," but in Japan, people simply say

Gochisoosama-deshita.

meaning "Thank you very much for everything you did to entertain me."

(January 9, 1977)

を可能にしてくれたすべての人、すべての物に対して向けられる。したがって、主人側への感謝の表明ともなるし、欧米での食前の祈りのような役割も果たす。

　食べ始めるようにと主人にうながされた時は、食べ始める前に「いただきます」と言うのが礼儀である。食べ終わったら「ごちそうさま」あるいはもっと丁寧に「ごちそうさまでした」と言う。すると主人側はこの賛辞を否定すべく、

　　おそまつさまでした

と言う。「気に入ってよかった」という言いかたは普通はしない。

　「ごちそうさま」について付け加えれば、これは単に食事に対する感謝ではなく、もてなし全体に対する感謝を表すものである。たとえばパーティーが終わって人の家を辞する時、米国人なら主人側の人に "Thank you very much. I had a wonderful time." と言うが、日本ではただ、

　　ごちそうさまでした

と言う。これは「おもてなしありがとうございました」の意味である。

(1977.1.9)

Mooshiwake arimasen
もうしわけ ありません
I'm very sorry

A few weeks ago Mr. Lerner forgot to bring a book that Mr. Takada had asked him to bring. He felt sorry about it and said

Doomo sumimasen.

(I'm very sorry.)

And Mr. Takada said politely *Iie, ii-n-desu-yo.* (No, that's all right.) but it was obvious that Mr. Lerner's negligence had inconvenienced him a great deal. So Mr. Lerner apologized again with a more polite expression

Hontoo-ni mooshiwake arimasen.

(I'm very sorry. —lit., I really have no apology to offer.)

Then Miss Yoshida who happened to be with them suddenly started laughing. When Mr. Lerner asked her what was so funny, she said that although he had apologized with polite expressions the way he had said them did not sound at all as if he was sorry. In fact, she said, he looked like a soldier reporting his actions to an officer.

Mr. Lerner suspected that his pronunciation was poor, so when he met Sensee a few days later he asked him about it.

No, Sensee said, it was not the pronunciation, but the bodily expression that was wrong. Mr. Lerner had said *Mooshiwake arimasen* (I'm very sorry) with his upper body held upright and with his chin up. That is not the way a Japanese would apologize, even to his friends.

申しわけありません

I'm very sorry

　数週間前のこと、Mr. Lerner は、Mr. Takada に頼まれた本を持ってくるのを忘れた。すまないと思ったので、

　　どうもすみません

と謝った。Mr. Takada はおだやかに、「いいえ、いいんですよ」と言ったが、Mr. Lerner の不注意のために大変な迷惑をこうむったのは明らかであった。そこで Mr. Lerner はもっと丁寧な表現で詫びた。

　　ほんとうに申しわけありません

すると、そばにいた Miss Yoshida が急に笑い出した。何がおかしいのかと聞くと、言葉そのものは丁寧だけど、態度が全然申しわけなさそうに見えないというのだ。彼女の言葉を借りると、まるで兵士が上官に報告を行っているようだとのことだった。

　Mr. Lerner は、発音がまずかったのかなと思ったので、2、3日あとで先生に会った時聞いてみた。

　いや、発音じゃない、と先生は言った。悪かったのは姿勢だったのだ。Mr. Lerner が「申しわけありません」と言った時、上半身がピンと張りあごが上がっていたのだろう。日本人が詫びる時の姿勢はそうではない。たとえ友人に対してでも、それではまずい、と先生は言った……。

*   *   *

Saying things in an inappropriate manner is not only ineffective but also likely to cause misunderstanding. Apologizing or making a request while standing straight and with the chin up will seem quite strange to the Japanese; it may even be offensive. A very fluent speaker of Japanese we know once experienced this kind of misunderstanding.

Japanese often bow or bend their upper body not only when apologizing or making a request but also when offering things. It is necessary to do so when offering sympathy to someone for his misfortune. You may have seen in person or in dramas how Japanese offer their condolences to a bereaved person. The set expression

Kono tabi-wa tonda koto-de gozaimashita.

(I'm very sorry to hear it. —lit., This time it was a terrible thing.)

is not said clearly to the end; usually people bow or look down saying just

Kono tabi-wa doomo . . .

(lit., This time indeed . . .)

and the rest is either mumbled or said inaudibly. In such cases bowing is as eloquent, or even more eloquent, than words.

(March 19, 1978)

＊　　　　　＊　　　　　＊

　ものを言う時の態度が適切でないと、意図もよく伝わらないし、誤解を生む恐れもある。体をまっすぐにし、あごを上向けて、非礼を詫びたり依頼をしたりするのは、日本人には奇妙に思われる。失礼でさえある。知人の中にも、流暢な日本語の使い手でありながら、この種の誤解を招いた人がいる。

　日本人は、詫びる時や依頼する時だけでなく、物をすすめる時にも、おじぎをしたり上半身をかがめたりすることが多い。人の不幸に対して同情の意を示す時も、そうする必要がある。実際に、あるいはドラマの中などで、日本人が家族を失った人にくやみを言っているのを見たかもしれないが、決まった表現、

　　　このたびは、とんだことでございました

は、終わりまではっきりと発音しない。普通はおじぎをしたり下を向いたりしながら、ただ、

　　　このたびは、どうも……

とだけ言って、あとは口の中でぶつぶつ言うか、聞こえないほど細い声で言う。こうした場合、おじぎをすることは、言葉によるくやみと同様に、いやそれ以上に、雄弁なのである。

(1978.3.19)

Soo-desu-ne
そうですね
Well . . .

Mr. Lerner listened while Mr. Takada was carefully explaining a proposal to Mr. Saito. Mr. Saito listened attentively, giving frequent *aizuchi*. When Mr. Takada had finished his explanation, Mr. Saito said

Soo-desu-ne.

Mr. Lerner thought this meant "That's right," and expected him to say *Ja, soo shimashoo.* But Mr. Saito said *Ja, moo ichido kangaete-mimasu* (I'll think it over), and left. Mr. Takada said that Mr. Saito would not accept their proposal. Mr. Lerner did not understand why he had said *Soo-desu-ne* first. But when he listened to Japanese talking, he noticed that they often start their replies with *Soo-desu-ne* regardless of what follows. They say

Soo-desu-ne. Yappari yamemashoo.
(lit., That's right. I won't do that.)
Soo-desu-ne. Yoku wakarimasen.
(lit., That's right. I don't understand it well.)

It seemed to Mr. Lerner that this *Soo-desu-ne* doesn't mean anything; it just shows that the speaker is going to give his reply.

*　　　　*　　　　*

そうですね

Well . . .

　Mr. Takada が Mr. Saito に向かって、注意深く企画を説明するのを、Mr. Lerner もそばで聞いていた。Mr. Saito は頻繁に相づちを打ちながら熱心に聞いていた。Mr. Takada が説明を終わると、Mr. Saito は、

　　　そうですね

と言った。

　Mr. Lerner はこれは "That's right." の意味だと思ったので、このあとすぐ「じゃ、そうしましょう」と続けるものと思った。ところが Mr. Saito は、「じゃ、もう一度考えてみます」と言って出て行った。Mr. Takada はこの企画には乗らないだろうと言った。Mr. Lerner はなぜ彼が始めに「そうですね」と言ったのか、理解できなかった。しかし、他の日本人の話を聞いてみると、次にくる言葉と関係なく、「そうですね」が使われることがわかった。たとえば、

　　　そうですね、やっぱりやめましょう
　　　そうですね、よくわかりません

Mr. Lerner には、この「そうですね」には何も意味がなく、これからお答えをしますという合図に過ぎないように思われた……。

＊　　　　　＊　　　　　＊

　「そうですね」は、話し手が相手の質問を理解し、これから答えようとしていることを示すものである（「ええ」や「はい」もよく用いられる）。この意味で

Soo-desu-ne is used to show that the speaker has understood what has been asked and is going to reply to it. (*Ee* and *Hai* are also often used in this way.) In this sense, it is similar to "Well" in such sentences as "Well, I think . . ." In polite speech Japanese use *Soo-desu-ne* and in familiar speech they say *Soo-da-ne* (male) or *Soo-ne* (usually female).

It is said in a different tone when it doesn't mean "That's right." When it means "That's right," it is said with a falling tone like

<pre>
So
    o
        -desu-ne.
</pre>

When it is used to solicit agreement, meaning "That's right, don't you think?", it is said with a rising tone on the *ne* as

<pre>
So
    o   -ne?
        -desu
</pre>

When it is used to mean "Well, . . ." it is said with a dangling tone as

<pre>
So
    o
        -desu-nee . . .
</pre>

This is different from *Eeto* although both can be translated as "Well." *Eeto* is used when one cannot think of the right word, while *Soo-desu-ne* is usually intentionally used to avoid the abruptness which might be caused by giving the answer immediately. To prove this, children seldom use *Soo-desu-ne* or *Soo-da-ne* but they often use *Eeto.*

(November 20, 1977)

は、"Well, I think ..." と言うような場合の "Well" に似ている。丁寧な話では「そうですね」と言い、くだけた会話では「そうだね」（男性）や「そうね」（おもに女性）を用いる。

　"That's right." の意味の時とは音調が異なる。"That's right." の意味では、

<pre>
　　　そ
　　　　　う
　　　　　　　ですね
</pre>

のように下り調子となる。"That's right, don't you think?" のように、相手の同意を求める時は「ね」が上がって、

<pre>
　　　そ
　　　　　う　　　　　ね！
　　　　　　　です
</pre>

となる。"Well ..." の意味の時はためらいがちな口調で、

<pre>
　　　そ
　　　　　う
　　　　　　　ですねえ……
</pre>

となる。

　これは「ええと」とは異なる。「ええと」も "Well" に当たるが、こちらは適当な語を考えている時に使うものであり、「そうですね」のほうは、ただちに答えを言うと唐突な感じがするのを避けるため、意図的に用いられるのである。その証拠に、子供は「そうですね」や「そうだね」は使わないが、「ええと」はよく用いている。

(1977.11.20)

Itte-(i)rasshai
いって（い）らっしゃい
Please go and come back

One morning when Mr. Lerner was hurrying to the station, his neighbor Mrs. Okada, who was sweeping the road in front of her house, said,

Itte-(i)rasshai.
(Have a nice day. —lit., Please go and come back.)

Mr. Lerner did not know how to respond to this greeting, so he just said *Sayoonara,* although he felt this was not quite right. Later at the office, Mr. Takada told him that he should have said

Itte-mairimasu or *Itte-kimasu.*
(Thank you, I will. —lit., I'll go and come back.)

*   *   *

Itte-(i)rasshai and *Itte-mairimasu* (or *Itte-kimasu*) are exchanged in a home when a family member leaves. It is customary for someone going out to say *Itte-mairimasu* or *Itte-kimasu* (less polite), and for those remaining to say *Itte-(i)rasshai.*

Those expressions are also used between non-family members when they feel that they belong to the same group. The concept of "group" differs in its range depending on the individual, but usually people living in a neighborhood or people working at the same company are regarded as members of a group. Thus, these expressions are used when a neighbor or

行って(い)らっしゃい

Please go and come back

　ある朝、Mr. Lerner が駅へ向かって急いでいると、家の前の道を掃いていたお隣の奥さんが、

　　　行っていらっしゃい

と言った。

　Mr. Lerner はどう答えていいかわからなかったので、ただ「サヨウナラ」と言ったが、それではよくないような気がした。会社に着いてから Mr. Takada に聞くと、

　　　行ってまいります

あるいは、

　　　行ってきます

と言うべきだったと言う……。

＊　　　　＊　　　　＊

　家族の一員が家を出る時は、「行って(い)らっしゃい」と「行ってまいります(行ってきます)」のあいさつを交換する。出て行くほうは「行ってまいります」(丁寧) または「行ってきます」と言い、家に残るほうは「行って(い)らっしゃい」と言う。

　このあいさつは、家族同士でなくても、同じ集団に属していると感じられる場

a member of a company leaves temporarily.

Sayoonara (Good-bye) is not used among family members unless they expect that they will not meet again. If a husband says to his wife *Sayoonara* when leaving, that means he is not going to live with her any more.

When a family member comes home, he says

Tadaima.

(I'm home. —lit., (I'm home) right now.)

And his family members say

Okaerinasai.

(Welcome home. —lit., You have come.)

In English, people use various expressions when leaving and coming home, but in Japan, set expressions are used for these occasions: such expressions as *Konnichiwa* (Good day), *Konbanwa* (Good evening) or *Sayoonara* are not used among family members.

(February 6, 1977)

合に用いられる。「集団」の範囲については、人によって考えかたが異なるが、通常、近所に住んでいる人や同じ会社で働いている人は、同一集団の一員と考えられる。したがって、近隣の人や会社の仲間が一時的にその場を離れる時は、こうしたあいさつが交わされるのである。

「さようなら」は、家族の間では用いない。用いるのは二度と会わないと考えた時だけである。夫が家を出る時妻に「さようなら」と言ったとすれば、それは夫婦の別れを意味する。

人が家に帰った時には、

　　　ただいま

と言い、家族は、

　　　お帰りなさい

と迎える。

英語では、家を出る時や戻った時に、さまざまな言葉を用いてあいさつするが、日本ではこの場合には決まったあいさつがあるわけである。「こんにちは」「こんばんは」「さようなら」などは、家族間では用いない。

(1977.2.6)

Makoto-ni tsumaranai mono-desu-ga . . .
まことに つまらない ものですが…
This is very little, but . . .

Mr. Lerner and Miss Yoshida were invited to the Takadas' last Saturday. Both of them brought a gift and handed it to Mrs. Takada. Mr. Lerner said politely

Makoto-ni tsumaranai mono-desu-ga . . .
(This is very little, but please accept it.)

and handed her a box of candy. Since the box was rather small, he used one hand to hand it over, but Mrs. Takada took it with two hands and thanked him very politely. And when Miss Yoshida handed over her gift, she held it in two hands although the package of fruit was not large, and Mrs. Takada again used two hands to take it. He wondered if he should have used two hands or if only women do so.

After that Mr. Lerner paid careful attention to how the Japanese hand things over, and found that they usually use two hands when they act politely, except when handing over very small things.

*   *   *

To hand something to someone politely, it is important that even when one hand is used to actually hand it over, the other hand also be used in the action; very often the other hand is placed on it or touches it slightly, as if to confirm the action of handing it over. Namely, when one hand is used to hand over something, the other hand should not be put into a

まことにつまらないものですが…

This is very little, but . . .

先週の土曜日、Mr. Lerner と Miss Yoshida は Takada 家に招かれた。2人とも手みやげを持っていって Mrs. Takada に渡した。Mr. Lerner は礼儀正しく、

　まことにつまらないものですが……

と言って、キャンデーの箱を手渡した。小さめの箱だったので、片手で持って渡したのだが、Mrs. Takada はそれを両手で受け取って、丁寧な口調で礼を述べた。次に Miss Yoshida が手みやげを渡す時、あまり大きくない果物の包みであったが両手で持って渡し、Mrs. Takada もまた両手で受け取った。Mr. Lerner は、自分も両手を使うべきだったのか、それともそうするのは女性だけだろうかと思った。

　その後、日本人が物を手渡す時にどのようにするか注意していたが、その結果わかったのは、丁寧な行動をとる時は、よほど小さなものは別として、両手を使うのが普通であるということだった……。

＊　　　　　＊　　　　　＊

　人に何かを丁寧に手渡す時大切なことは、手渡すこと自体に使われるのが片手であっても、もう一方の手もその行為に参加していることである。もう一方の手を渡す物の上にのせたり、軽く品物にふれたりして、手渡すという行為をたしかめるような形をとることが多い。すなわち、何かを渡す時に使うのは一方の手であっても、もう一方の手をポケットにつっこんでいたり、脇にだらりと下げてい

pocket or by one's side.

Politeness has to be supported by consideration to the recipient; the recipient has to be able to take the thing in a proper, easy and pleasant way. For example, when handing over a book or a letter one has to hand it so that the recipient can read it; the recipient should be able to use such things as scissors or pens from the moment they have been handed to him.

The angle is also important; when handing over something with a square shape, one should hand it so that the recipient can take it squarely, not diagonally.

Verbal expressions have to be accompanied by the appropriate non-verbal action. When one uses such polite verbal expressions as *Makoto-ni tsumaranai mono-desu-ga . . .* one also has to use the appropriate polite action; otherwise the recipient will be embarrassed and not know how to respond.

(April 19, 1981)

Anata
あなた
You

Mr. Lerner was talking with Mr. Mori, the director of his company. When he said

Anata-mo ikimasu-ka.

(Are you going, too?)

たのではいけないのである。

　礼儀を支えるのは、受け取り手に対する思いやりの心である。受け取る側が適切な、無理のない、気持ちのよい形で受け取ることができるようにしなければならない。たとえば本や手紙を渡す時は、受け取る人がすぐ読めるように渡すべきであるし、はさみやペンの場合は、受け取った人がすぐそのまま使うことができるようにしなければならない。

　手渡す角度も大切である。四角の形をしたものを手渡す時は、斜めに向けず正面から受け取ってもらうようにする。

　言葉のあいさつと身のこなしは、よく合ったものでなければならない。「まことにつまらない物ですが」のような丁寧な言葉を述べる時は、行動も丁寧にすることである。そうでないと、受け取り手は困ってしまって、どう応じてよいかわからなくなる。

(1981.4.19)

あなた

You

Mr. Lerner が社長の Mr. Mori と歓談中、ふと、

　　アナタモ　行キマスカ

と言ったところ、しばらく社長の答えがなかった。Mr. Lerner を見つめてから、

Mr. Mori did not reply for a moment. He looked at Mr. Lerner and then said "yes" coldly. Afterward, Mr. Takada, who was present then, told Mr. Lerner that it was not polite to call the director *anata*.

After this, Mr. Lerner paid careful attention to how *anata* is used by Japanese, and found it to be rather unpopular among them. It was surprising to learn how infrequently it is used compared with "you," its apparent English equivalent.

*　　　　*　　　　*

The Japanese very often do without any personal pronouns; indeed Japanese seem to avoid using them. When they have to use some word to refer to a person, they use personal names instead of the personal pronouns corresponding to "he," "she," or "you" in English. It is sometimes impossible to judge whether the speaker is talking about the second or third person from just looking at the sentence itself. For example, *Mori-san-mo ikimasu-ka* literally means "Is Mr. Mori going, too?" but in practice it can mean "Are you going, too?"

Sometimes the names of positions are used instead of personal names. Such terms as *sensee* (teacher), *shachoo* (director), *okusan* (wife), and *okaasan* (mother) are used in place of the name or *anata*. Especially when the position deserves respect, its name should be used rather than the personal name or *anata*. Thus Mr. Lerner should have said *Shachoo-mo irasshai-masu-ka* to his director instead of *Anata-mo ikimasu-ka*. (The verb must be chosen according to the level of politeness, so *irasshaimasu* is used instead of *ikimasu*.)

Anata is used in a very limited way. It can be used by older people to younger people. A teacher can call his student *anata*, but a student should not call his teacher *anata*. A mother can say *Anata-mo iku?* to her child (*Iku* is the non-polite form of *ikimasu*), but the child never uses the same

冷たい口調で「ええ」と言う。その場に居合わせた Mr. Takada があとになって、「社長をアナタと呼ぶのは失礼だ」と教えてくれた。

　そのあと日本人の話を注意して聞いていると、「あなた」がどうも不人気であることがわかった。英語の "you" にくらべるとその頻度の低さは驚くばかりであった……。

＊　　　　　　＊　　　　　　＊

　日本語では人称代名詞なしで済ませることが多く、人称代名詞の使用を避けているような印象がある。誰のことを言っているか明らかにする必要がある時は、"he," "she," "you" に当たる語の代わりに、人名を用いる。時には、文の形だけでは、二人称のことか三人称について言っているのか不明の場合もある。たとえば、「森さんも行きますか」の文字通りの意味は、"Is Mr. Mori going, too?" であるが、実際には "Are you going, too?" の意味を持つこともある。

　時には地位の名称が代わりに用いられる。「先生」「社長」「奥さん」「お母さん」などが、「あなた」の代わりに使われるのである。特にその地位が敬意に値するものであれば、姓名や「あなた」に優先して用いられる。したがって、Mr. Lerner は社長に対して、「アナタモ行キマスカ」ではなく、「社長もいらっしゃいますか」と言うべきであった。（敬意に応じて動詞を選ぶので、「行きます」ではなく「いらっしゃいます」を使う。）

　「あなた」が用いられる場合は、極めて限られている。年長者が年下の者に対して用いることは良い。教師が学生を「あなた」と呼ぶのは差し支えないが、学生が教師を「あなた」と呼んではならない。母親が子供に対して「あなたも行く？」（「行く」は「行きます」に対する非丁寧形）と言うのはよいが、子供が同じ文を母親に向かって用いることはあり得ない。

　「あなた」は同年配の女性の間でも用いられる。（同じ場面で男性は「君」または「お前」を使う。）この場合も、影の薄い「あなた」は人名や地位の名称に押しやられてしまう。2 人の主婦が話し合うとしたら、次のようになる率が高い。

sentence to his mother.

Anata is also used among women of the same age. (Men use *kimi* or *omae* in the same situation.) Here, too, the vulnerable *anata* is liable to be replaced by personal names or the names of positions. Two housewives are very likely to say,

A: *Okusan-mo iku?* (lit., Is the wife going, too?)
B: *Ee, okusan-mo?* (lit., Yes. The wife, too?)

This exchange actually means "Are you going, too?" and "Yes. You, too?"

(Octoberf 10, 1976)

'Makoto'-to 'Kobayashi-san'
「まこと」と「小林さん」
'Makoto' vs. 'Kobayashi-san'

Mr. Makoto Kobayashi is the youngest worker in the office where Mr. Lerner works. Although people call each other by their last names at work, Mr. Kobayashi is called "Makoto" as if he were everybody's younger brother.

The other day Mr. Lerner and several other colleagues were invited to the Kobayashi house. Makoto's parents welcomed them warmly and expressed their thanks to them for being kind to Makoto. After dinner, when having tea together, Mr. Lerner wanted to say something nice about Makoto and started saying

A：奥さんも行く？

B：ええ。奥さんも？

これで実際の意味は、"Are you going, too?" "Yes. You, too?" に当たるのである。

(1976.10.10)

「まこと」と「小林さん」

'Makoto' vs. 'Kobayashi-san'

　Mr. Makoto Kobayashi は、Mr. Lerner のつとめている会社の最年少社員である。職場では互いに人の姓を呼ぶのに、Mr. Kobayashi だけは「まこと」と呼ばれている。ちょうど全員の弟のように思われているからであろう。

　この間 Mr. Lerner と数人の同僚が Mr. Kobayashi の家に招かれた。彼の両親はお客を歓待し、息子がお世話になっていると礼を述べた。夕食が終わってお茶を飲んでいた時、Mr. Lerner は Makoto のよいところをほめようと思って、

Makoto-wa totemo yoku hataraku-n-desu.

(Makoto is a very hard worker.)

But the parents did not seem to like this. While Mr. Lerner was wondering if he should go on or not, Miss Yoshida hurriedly added, as if to cover Mr. Lerner's blunder

Kobayashi-san-wa . . .

Mr. Lerner realized then that he had been rude in saying "Makoto" without any term of respect.

*   *   *

The use of terms of respect varies according to the situation; a term that is appropriate within a group will not always be appropriate in another situation. Mr. Kobayashi is called "Makoto" by his colleagues, but he has to be referred to differently when he is in another group. When referring to him in his parents' presence, his position as their son must be considered. Calling him "Makoto" in the presence of his parents sounds as if Makoto is not valued very highly by his colleagues.

This distinction between "in-group" terms and "out-group" terms is strictly observed. A male high school teacher will usually call his students by their last names without terms of respect as "Yoshida," "Takahashi," etc. But when he talks with their parents he will use *kun* with either the last name or the first name of the male students and *san* with those of the female students.

(June 14, 1981)

　　マコトハトテモヨク働クンデス

と言いかけたが、彼の両親はそれを聞いてあまり喜ばないようだった。話を続けようかやめようかと迷っていると、Miss Yoshida がそれを取りなすかのように、

　　小林さんは……

と言い出した。Mr. Lerner は、自分が「マコト」と呼びすてにしたのは失礼だったのだと悟った……。

＊　　　　　　＊　　　　　　＊

　敬称の用いかたは場合によって変わってくる。ある集団の中では適切な呼びかたも、別の場面では適切でなくなる。Mr. Kobayashi は会社の仲間には「まこと」と呼ばれているが、別の集団に入れば別の呼びかたをされる。彼の両親のいるところで呼ぶ時は、彼らの息子としての立場を考えなければならない。両親の前で「まこと」と呼ぶのは、彼が同僚にあまり重く見られていないという印象を与えることになる。

　「集団内」の呼称と「集団外」の呼称とは、きびしく区別しなければならない。男性の高校教師などは、通常自分の学生に対して姓を呼びすてにして、「吉田」とか「高橋」のように言う。しかしその学生の両親と話す時には、姓にせよ名にせよ呼びすてにせず、男子学生なら「君」を、女子学生なら「さん」をつけて呼ぶ。

(1981.6.14)

Senjitsu-wa gochisoosama-deshita
先日は ごちそうさまでした
Thank you for the treat the other day

The other day Mr. Lerner met Mr. Saito after about two months. Mr. Saito greeted him by saying,

Senjitsu-wa gochisoosama-deshita.

(Thank you for the treat the other day.)

Mr. Lerner was surprised that Mr. Saito referred to their previous meeting that had taken place quite a while before; and he was even more surprised when he remembered that he had only bought him a cup of coffee at a coffee shop. It did not seem to be worth Mr. Saito's expressing gratitude again after two months.

But when he started thinking about it, he realized that almost everyone said the same thing as Mr. Saito had. He could not help wondering if one has to have a good memory in order to be polite in Japan.

*   *   *

The answer to Mr. Lerner's question is yes. A Japanese has to remember and express gratitude for the favors received at the last meeting. You might think it is not necessary because you already thanked him adequately at the time, but it is customary to do so in Japan and is bad manners not to do so.

This custom may give you the impression that Japanese are overly conscious of the money they spend to treat others, but that is not the case. It

先日はごちそうさまでした

Thank you for the treat the other day

Mr. Lerner が先日、2か月ぶりに Mr. Saito に会ったところ、Mr. Saito はまず、

先日はごちそうさまでした

とあいさつした。

Mr. Lerner は驚いた。前回会ったのはずいぶん前のことだし、ごちそうさまといっても喫茶店でコーヒーをおごっただけである。2か月もたってからお礼を言われるほどのことではない。

しかし考えてみると、大抵の人が Mr. Saito と同じようなことを言う。日本では礼儀正しくあるためには、よほど記憶力がよくないといけないのかと Mr. Lerner は考えこんだ……。

＊　　　　　＊　　　　　＊

Mr. Lerner の疑問に対する答えは yes である。前回の会合で受けた好意は必ず記憶にとどめて、礼を述べる必要がある。その時十分に感謝の意を表したのだから、もう一度礼を述べる必要はないと思われるかもしれないが、日本ではこれが慣例であって、怠ってはならないことである。

この習慣の話を聞くと、日本人は人にごちそうした費用にこだわるからだと思われるかもしれないが、実はそうではない。どちらが金を払ったかということよりは、前回会って楽しかったという事実を記憶していることが重要なのである。金銭的な授受がなかった時でも、前回の出会いに言及すべきであって、その場合

is important to remember your meeting and having a good time together rather than who treated whom. You should refer to the previous meeting even when there was no giving and receiving of favors; in such cases you are supposed to say

Senjitsu-wa shitsuree-shimashita.

(I was rude the last time we met.)

instead of *Senjitsu-wa gochisoosama-deshita.*

What really counts is to show that you and the listener remember sharing the same experience; the memory of having the same experience helps to establish good relations between the two of you. Japanese consider it essential to start by establishing good relations before getting down to business. That is why this expression is used as a greeting when an English-speaking person would say "How have you been?" or just "Hello."

We have heard quite a few Japanese complain that their American acquaintances do not follow this custom: some of them even think it is rude.

(December 12, 1976)

Shujin-ga osewa-ni natte-orimasu
主人が おせわに なっております
Thank you for taking care of my husband

When Mr. Lerner was introduced to Mrs. Takada, the wife of his co-worker, she said,

には「先日はごちそうさまでした」でなく、

　　　先日は失礼しました

と言う。

　大事なのは、自分と相手が同じ経験を分かち合ったことを忘れていないということを示すことである。同じ経験を持ったことの記憶が両者の良い関係を築くのに役立つ。だからこそ、英語の社会で "How have you been?" とか "Hello" と言うような場面で、この表現が使われるのである。

　日本人の中には、アメリカ人の知り合いがこの習慣を守ってくれないと残念がる者も少なくない。時には、礼儀知らずだとまで言う場合もある。

(1976.12.12)

主人がお世話になっております

Thank you for taking care of my husband

Mr. Lerner が同僚 Mr. Takada の奥さんに紹介された時、奥さんは、

Shujin-ga itsumo osewa-ni natte-orimasu.

(lit., My husband is always taken care of by you.)

Mr. Lerner did not exactly understand what she had said, but guessed that she was thanking him for something he had done for her husband, and simply said *Iie* in reply.

Later he learned that *Iie* was all right but that *Kochira-koso* is the most appropriate answer.

*   *   *

Osewa-ni naru literally means "to be taken care of." *Shujin-ga osewa-ni natte-orimasu* sounds strange if translated literally, but this expression is actually used to mean "Thank you for your kindnesses to my husband." It is customary to use this expression when introduced to an acquaintance of one's family members. Just as a wife says *Shujin-ga . . .* , a husband says *Kanai-ga . . .* (My wife . . .) and parents say *Kodomo-ga . . .* (My child . . .) (or they mention the name of their child such as *Kazuo-ga . . .*) Parents use this expression without fail towards their child's teacher or doctor.

As is true with other expressions, this expression too can be used simply as a formality. A wife may say *Shujin-ga osewa-ni natte-orimasu* when she is really grateful as well as when she feels that the listener does not particularly deserve her gratitude.

We can see two important underlying ideas behind this expression. One is that the Japanese feel it essential to express their gratitude for favors done for their family members just as if they had received them themselves. Another idea is that the state of being associated with someone should be regarded as *osewa-ni naru* because one may be receiving favors from him even if one doesn't realize it at the time.

(March 27, 1977)

　　　主人がいつもお世話になっております

と言った。

　正確な意味はわからなかったが、何か夫のことでお礼を言っているのだと思ったので、ただ「いいえ」と答えておいた。

　あとになって聞いたところでは、「いいえ」でもよいが、「こちらこそ」が最も適切な答えだったそうである……。

*　　　　　*　　　　　*

　「お世話になる」は文字通りには "to be taken care of" の意味であるから、「主人がお世話になっております」を直訳すると、おかしなことになってしまう。しかしこのあいさつは、実際には "Thank you for your kindnesses to my husband." の意味で使われているのである。家族の知り合いに紹介された時は、このあいさつをするのが習慣である。「主人が……」と言うのと同じように、夫は「家内が……」と言い、親は「子供が……」（あるいは「一夫が……」のように子供の名前を使う）と言う。親は子供の先生や医者には必ずこう言う。

　他のあいさつでも同じであるが、このあいさつも、単に形式的に用いられる場合がある。妻が「主人がお世話になっております」と言う時は、心から感謝している場合もあれば、礼を言う必要はないと感じながら言う場合もある。

　この言葉の底には2つの重要な観念が秘められている。ひとつは、家族に対する好意に対しては、自分自身が好意を受けたのと同じように、感謝の意を示すべきだという考えである。他のひとつは、人とのつながりは、自覚しなくも恩恵をこうむっているかもしれないから、「お世話になる」という関係でとらえるべきだ、という考えである。

(1977.3.27)

Chapter 2

Mutual Understanding and Self-expression

相互理解と自己表現

It is not easy, although essential to living in society, to state one's wishes or standpoint so that others can easily accept them or at least correctly understand them. This chapter shows how the Japanese try hard to find appropriate expressions for this purpose.

We introduce here expressions corresponding to the English "Probably I shouldn't say this, but" or "I hate to say this, but"—used to start speaking—and to "I don't mean to say that I can't, but" or "I'm sorry, but"—used to tell someone that you cannot meet their wishes. Also, we explain how the Japanese ask about another's wishes or situations with appropriate reserve; direct questions like *Nomitai-desu-ka* (Do you want to drink it?) or *Wakarimashita-ka* (Did you understand?) can jeopardize human relations when used without discretion.

Also, we discussed such expressions as *Naruhodo* (Indeed), used to show agreement, and *. . . to yuu-to* (So . . . ?), *De, kyoo-wa* (Well, what can I do for you today?) to find out what the other person really wants to say; these expressions show how the painstaking efforts Japanese make in speech. *Guchi-o yuu* shows how Japanese businessmen get together after work at restaurants and beer halls to complain and listen to the complaints of their colleagues to comfort each other.

　相手に受けいれられやすいように自己の希望や事情を述べること、ま
た正しい理解を得ることは、社会生活の上で必要ではあるが決して容易
なことではない。この章では自己の欲求を示すための表現と相手を理解
するための適切な表現に日本人が心をくだいていることを示す例を集め
ている。

　言いにくいことを言い出す前の「こんなことを言ってはなんですが」
「言いにくいんですが」のような切り出しかたの用法、相手の希望に添
えないことを告げる「できないわけじゃありませんけど……」「申しわ
けありませんが、あのう……」のような遠慮深い表現を紹介している。
また、直接に相手の希望や状態をたずねることがはばかられる場合のあ
ることを示すものとして「飲みたいですか」「わかりましたか」など、
不用意に用いると相手との関係を傷つける可能性のある発言についての
説明も示している。

　また、相手に賛同するときの「なるほど」の用いかた、相手の真に言
いたいことを聞き出すための「……というと」「で、きょうは……？」
などのような表現に日本人の苦心がふくまれていることも興味深い。一
日の仕事のあとでバーやレストランに集まってぐちを言いあう人々の気
持ちを分析した「ぐちを言う」には、ことばに示された社会の一面を見
ることができよう。

To yuu-to . . .
と いう と…
So . . . ?

A few weeks ago Miss Yoshida asked Mr. Lerner if he would be able to come to a party at her house on Saturday. Mr. Lerner had made plans to go to Kyoto on that day, so he said,

Sono hi-wa ikemasen. To yuu-to Kyooto-e ikanakereba narimasen.

meaning "I won't be able to come on that day. The reason is that I must go to Kyoto." He had learned the expression *to yuu-to* which he understood is used before explaining what preceded. Miss Yoshida understood what he meant, but she said that *to yuu-to* somehow seemed strange.

Mr. Takada agreed with her and said that Mr. Lerner should have used *to yuu-no-wa* instead when stating the reason for what he had said. He added that *to yuu-to* is used when asking someone else to give a reason.

*   *   *

The two expressions are fundamentally used for different purposes. *To yuu-no-wa* (which literally means "To say . . . is") is used when giving the reason for the preceding statement. On the other hand *to yuu-to* (literally "when you say . . ." or "when I say . . .") is used to continue or develop the preceding statement; it corresponds to the English "so . . ." or "so . . . ?"

But in actual usage these two expressions give quite different impressions. Suppose someone has said that he won't be able to come on a certain

というと…

So . . . ?

　2、3週間前のこと、Miss Yoshida が、土曜日に家でパーティーをするから来てくれないかと言ったが、Mr. Lerner はその日は京都へ行く予定があったので、

　　　　ソノ日ハ行ケマセン。トイウト京都へ行カナケレバナリマセン

と答えた。

　「〜。というと」というのは、すでに言ったことの説明をする前につけるものだと習ったからである。Miss Yoshida は、意味はわかるけれど、ここで「というと」を使うのは、何だか変だと言った。

　Mr. Takada も賛成して、理由を説明するなら「〜。というのは」を使うべきだったと言った。さらに、「というと」は他の人に理由の説明を求める時に使うのだ、とつけ加えた……。

＊　　　　　　＊　　　　　　＊

　この2つの表現は基本的に違う目的に用いられる。「〜。というのは」は、前に述べたことについて、その理由を説明するものであり、一方「〜。というと」は、前の話をさらに続けたり発展させたりしたい時に用いられる。英語で表すと、"So . . ." あるいは "So . . . ?" に当たる。

　実際の用法では、この2つは全く違った印象を与える。たとえばだれかが、ある特定の日に来られないと言うので、その理由をたずねるとする。次の2つの会話は、文法的にはどちらも正しいが、丁寧さの点でやや違いがある。

day and you want to know why. The following two conversations are both correct grammatically but there is some difference in politeness.

I.   A: *Sono hi-wa korarenai-n-desu-ga.*

(I won't be able to come on that day.)

B: *To yuu-no-wa …?*

A: *Kyooto-e iku-n-desu.* (I'm going to Kyoto.)

II. A: *Sono hi-wa korarenai-n-desu-ga.*

B: *To yuu-to …?*

A: *Kyooto-e iku-n-desu.*

Speaker B may sound impolite in I. Since *to yuu-no-wa* is used to directly ask for the reason, it tends to sound demanding. In social situations it is usually replaced by *to yuu-to* even when one wishes to know the reason. And in this case *to iimasu-to* or *to osshaimasu-to* is used to sound more polite.

Saying *to yuu-no-wa …?* sounds like bluntly asking "Why?" as in a police detective examining a suspect or a teacher asking a student to prove the validity of his answer. It should be especially avoided when the question concerns something that the speaker may not want to talk about. And, to be more polite, one should just say

Soo-desu-ka.

(Is that so?)

or

Haa … haa.

(Yes … ?)

and wait for the other to start giving the reason.

(April 16, 1978)

　Ⅰ　　A：その日は来られないんですが

　　　　B：というのは……？

　　　　A：京都へ行くんです

　Ⅱ　　A：その日は来られないんですが

　　　　B：というと……？

　　　　A：京都へ行くんです

ⅠのほうのBは失礼に聞こえるかもしれない。「というのは」は直接に理由をたずねるのに用いられているため、高圧的にひびきやすい。相手に気を使う場面では、理由を知りたいと思う場面でも、「というと」を使うのが普通である。そしてこの場合、もっと丁寧な話しかたとしては、「といいますと」や「とおっしゃいますと」などを使う。

　「というのは」を使うと、警察官が容疑者を尋問する時や、教師が学生に答えの正しさを証明させる時のような、ぶっきらぼうな印象を与える。まして相手が話したくないと思っていることを聞こうとするような場合には、特につつしむべき表現である。なお、もっと丁寧な話しかたでは、ただ、

　　　そうですか

とか、

　　　はあ……はあ

と言うだけで、相手が理由を言い始めるのを待つという態度がとられる。

（1978.4.16）

Naruhodo
なるほど
Indeed

Yesterday afternoon Mr. Mori, the director of the company where Mr. Lerner works, was explaining his plan. While listening to him, Mr. Lerner took special care to give *aizuchi* as often as he could. In the past few weeks he has become used to giving *aizuchi,* although not without some effort. This time, he wanted to use some expression other than *Hai, Ee,* or *Soo-desu-ka,* so he said

Naruhodo.

whenever Mr. Mori paused.

But Mr. Mori did not seem to like this. In fact when Mr. Lerner repeated this expression as *Naruhodo, naruhodo,* he stopped talking and asked him to listen quietly.

Mr. Lerner did not understand what was wrong with his use of *Naruhodo.* Don't Japanese use it very often, especially when listening to others explain things? And even when speaking English, many Japanese seem to say "I see" much too often, perhaps because they regard it as the English equivalent of *Naruhodo.*

*   *   *

The word *naruhodo* means "indeed," "it's true," or "surely," and is used to show that the speaker has understood perfectly what he has heard. In

なるほど

Indeed

　昨日の午後、Mr. Lerner の勤めている会社で、社長の Mr. Mori から、企画の説明があった。Mr. Lerner はできるだけ頻繁に相づちを打つように心がけた。この数週間で、苦労はするがなんとか相づちは打てるようになっていた。今回はいつもの「はい」「ええ」「そうです」とは違うものを使ってみたくなったので、Mr. Mori の句切れごとに、

　　　なるほど

とやった。

　しかし Mr. Mori はそれが気にいらないようだった。Mr. Lerner の「なるほど」「なるほど」がしばらく続くと、話しやめて、「黙って聞いてくれ」と Mr. Lerner に言った。

　なぜ「なるほど」がいけないのか、Mr. Lerner にはわからなかった。日本人はよく「なるほど」を使うし、特に説明を聞く時にはさかんに言うではないか。英語を話す時も、日本人は "I see." が多すぎるが、それは「なるほど」に当たるものとして使っているからではないのだろうか……。

＊　　　　＊　　　　＊

　「なるほど」は「全くその通り」「たしかに」の意味で、聞いたことを完全に理解したということを示す。この意味では相づちとして適当なのであるが、丁寧な話では使うのによほどの注意が必要である。

this sense it is an appropriate word to be used as *aizuchi,* but one has to be very careful when using it in polite speech.

Naruhodo belongs to a group of expressions which are used in a mono-logue-like way in polite speech, such as *Aa, soo-ka,* or *Aa, soo yuu wake-ka.* When the speaker uses these expressions in the midst of polite conver-sation, he has to show that they are directed to himself rather than to the listener. In other words, he is permitted to use in polite conversation ex-pressions that are originally familiar only when he is talking to himself. To show this, one has to pronounce such expressions with a lower tone and with a falling intonation; otherwise these expressions sound impolite.

Sometimes people use such expressions on purpose to show their en-thusiasm for the conversation. Interviewers on radio or TV programs, for example, often say *Naruhodo* to show that they are so absorbed in the con-versation that they have forgotten to pay attention to formalities; by doing this, they can encourage those they are interviewing. (Men use *Naruhodo* in this way more often than women; perhaps women are, or have been so far, trained to refrain from talking to themselves in public.)

Before you are used to this kind of speech, it might be safer to use *Soo-desu-ka* or *Wakarimashita* in polite speech instead of *Naruhodo,* and use such expressions as

Naruhodo, naruhodo.

or

Naruhodo-nee.

only in familiar conversations.

(January 15, 1978)

「なるほど」は、「です」「ます」調の話の中で独白的に言う「ああ、そうか」「ああ、そういうわけか」などに似ている。丁寧な話の中でこうした言葉を使う時は、相手に向けているのではなく、自分自身に向けて言っていることを明らかにしなければならない。丁寧な話の中でくだけた表現を用いるのは、ひとりごとの場合にしか許されないからである。この区別をはっきりさせるために、こうした表現は調子を落とし、下降型のイントネーションで言う。そうしないと、失礼な印象を与えるのである。

時には、話に夢中になっているという印象を与えるために、わざとこうした表現を用いることがある。ラジオやテレビ番組のインタビューなど、話の面白さに敬意を忘れたということを示すために「なるほど」を頻発することも多い。相手の話を誘い出す効果をねらっているわけである。（この用法は女性より男性に多い。おそらく女性は人前の話ではあまりひとりごとを言わないように、しつけられてきたからであろう。）

こうした話しかたに十分慣れるまでは、丁寧な話では「なるほど」を避けて、「そうですか」「わかりました」などを用いたほうが安全であろう。特に、

　　なるほど、なるほど

や、

　　なるほどねえ

は、くだけた話し合いの時だけにしたほうが賢明である。

（1978.1.15）

Konna koto-o itte-wa nan-desu-ga
こんな ことを いっては なんですが
Probably I shouldn't say this, but

A few days ago Mr. Lerner was chatting with Mr. Okada and several other people after a business discussion. Mr. Kato smoked a lot in the room and the air became rather bad. After Mr. Kato left the room Mr. Lerner started to open the window. Then Mr. Okada said,

Konna koto-o itte-wa nan-desu-ga.

(lit., Saying such a thing is what, but.)

While Mr. Lerner was wondering what *nan-desu-ga* meant, Mr. Okada continued and said that Mr. Kato should have asked the others for permission to smoke.

The next day, before he found out the meaning of the phrase *nan-desu-ga*, Miss Yoshida came to him and asked him to correct her letter in English to her pen pal, saying

Konna koto-o onegai-shite-wa nan-desu-kedo.

(lit., Asking such a thing is what.)

*   *   *

The expression *nan-desu-ga* or *nan-desu-kedo* means "it's something I shouldn't do." *Konna koto-o itte-wa nan-desu-ga* means "This is something I shouldn't say, but"; this is said before venturing some criticism. Before asking a favor which seems too big or too irrelevant, one says *Konna koto-o*

こんなことを言ってはなんですが

Probably I shouldn't say this, but

　２、３日前、仕事の話がすんで、Mr. Lerner は Mr. Okada たちと雑談していたが、Mr. Kato が続けざまにたばこを吸ったため、部屋の空気が汚くなった。Mr. Kato が部屋を出てから Mr. Lerner が窓を開けようとしていると、Mr. Okada が、

　　　こんなことを言ってはなんですが

と言った。「なんですが」というのはどういう意味だろうと考えていると、Mr. Okada は言葉を続けて、Mr. Kato はたばこを吸ってもいいかどうか他の人たちにたずねるべきだった、と言った。

　次の日、まだ「なんですが」の意味を調べないうちに、Miss Yoshida が、ペンフレンドに出す英語の手紙を持ってきて、

　　　こんなことをお願いしてはなんですけど

と言った……。

＊　　　　　＊　　　　　＊

　「なんですが」「なんですけど」は「するべきではないことだが」の意味である。「こんなことを言ってはなんですが」は、「これは言うべきではないのだが」の意味で、思い切って人の批判をする時などの前置きとして用いられる。あつかましい、あるいは筋違いと思われる依頼を持ちこむ時には、「こんなことをお願

onegai-shite-wa nan-desu-ga meaning "This is something I shouldn't ask you, but." Sometimes *nan-desu-kedo* is used by itself to show one's hesitation as in

Anoo . . . nan-desu-kedo, jitsu-wa . . .
(Excuse me, . . . well, as a matter of fact . . .)

Especially in polite conversation it is regarded as good to show hesitation before giving criticism. The following expressions might be useful:

Konna koto-wa itte-wa ikenai-to omoimasu-ga.
(I know I shouldn't say such a thing, but.)
Watashi-no omoichigai-kamo shiremasen-ga.
(I may be wrong, but.)

(April 1, 1979)

Iinikui-n-desu-ga
いいにくいんですが
I hate to say this, but

Last week Mr. Lerner took a proposal to the director of the company, Mr. Mori. Before he started explaining it to Mr. Mori and several other people, he thought that it might be hard to understand because of his inadequate Japanese, and said

Kore-wa taihen iinikui-n-desu-ga.

いしてはなんですが」と言う。

時には、「なんですけど」だけでためらいを表すこともある。

あのう、なんですけど、実は……

のように言う。

とくに丁寧な会話では、批判を口にする前に躊躇を示すのが礼儀である。このような場合には、

こんなことは、言ってはいけないと思いますが

とか、

わたしの思い違いかもしれませんが

などと言う。

(1979.4.1)

言いにくいんですが

I hate to say this, but

先週 Mr. Lerner は社長である Mr. Mori のところへ、計画書を持っていった。社長ほか数人の人たちの前で説明を始めようとした時、自分の不十分な日本語では理解するのが大変だろうと思ったので、「説明しにくい」の意味で、

コレハ大変言イニクインデスガ

meaning "This is very hard to explain, but." He expected this remark to be accepted with pleasure, but on the contrary the audience looked rather unpleasant, and some of them even looked stern.

So, Mr. Lerner added that his Japanese wouldn't be good enough; then the audience looked relieved and smiled.

Later Mr. Takada told him that he should have said

Umaku setsumee-dekinai-kamo shiremasen-ga.

(lit., I may not be able to explain it very well, but.)

instead.

*　　　　　*　　　　　*

To mean "hard to . . ." *nikui* is added to the stem of the verb as in *wakarinikui* (hard to understand) or *yominikui* (hard to read). Therefore it is grammatically correct to say *iinikui* to mean "hard to say," but *iinikui* in the above context usually means "I hate to say" or "I know I shouldn't say this."

Taihen iinikui-n-desu-ga.

is usually said before asking for a big favor or venturing some criticism. Therefore the audience looked prepared for some unpleasant remark when Mr. Lerner said this. (*Iinikui* can mean something else in another context; when one says *iinikui* to refer to a word, it means that the word is difficult to pronounce.)

The antonym of *wakarinikui* is *wakariyasui*; *yomiyasui hon* means "a book easy to read." We sometimes hear English speakers say

yasashiku kowaremasu

と言った。こう言ったら喜んで聞いてもらえると思ったのだが、聞き手はむしろ不愉快な顔つきになり、中にはひたいにしわを寄せた人もいた。

そこで Mr. Lerner は、自分の日本語力が不十分なので、とつけ加えた。すると人々はほっとした様子で顔をほころばせた。

あとで Mr. Takada にきくと、

　　うまく説明できないかもしれませんが

と言えばよかったのだそうである……。

＊　　　　　＊　　　　　＊

「〜はむずかしい」という意味を表すには「にくい」をつけて、「わかりにくい」「読みにくい」などと言う。「言うのがむずかしい」という意味を表すのに「言いにくい」とするのは、文法的には間違っていないが、上記のような場面では、「言いたくないが」とか「こんなこと、言うべきではないが」の意味になるのが普通である。

　　大変言いにくいんですが

というのは、通常大きな願いごとを述べる時か、思い切って批判をする時の前置きである。それで Mr. Lerner がこう言った時、聞いていた人たちは、何か不愉快な話が出るのだろうと思って身構えたのである。（「言いにくい」には、文脈によっては他の意味もある。特定の語について「言いにくい」と言うのは、「発音しにくい」の意味である。）

「わかりにくい」の反対は「わかりやすい」である。「読みやすい本」などと言う。英語を話す人の中には、「こわれやすい」を、

　　ヤサシクコワレマス

と言ったり、「おぼえやすい」を、

to mean *kowareyasui* (easy to break) or

yasashiku oboemasu

for *oboeyasui* (easy to learn). These expressions are strange because *yasashiku* usually means "tenderly" or "gently" rather than "easily."

(February 11, 1979)

Okyakusan
おきゃくさん
Visitor

A few days ago Mr. Lerner dropped in at a little drugstore to buy something. When he was about to leave, the woman called out to him saying

Okyakusan, wasuremono-desu-yo.
(You've left something, sir.)

Mr. Lerner thanked her and picked up the package he had forgotten to take. He realized then that the word *okyakusan* which means "visitor" is used to refer to a customer, too.

On the following day, when he was waiting on the platform for the train, he heard a station employee address one of the passengers as *Okyakusan*. A passenger, he learned, is also called *okyakusan*.

ヤサシクオボエマス

と言ったりする人があるが、これは異様に聞こえる。「やさしく」は通常「容易に」ではなく、「ものやわらかに」「おだやかに」の意味に用いられるからである。

(1979.2.11)

お客さん

Visitor

　2、3日前のこと、Mr. Lerner はある小さな薬局でちょっと買い物をした。店を出ようとすると、女性の店員が呼びとめて、

　　お客さん、忘れ物ですよ

と言った。礼を述べて、置き忘れた包みをとったが、その時、「訪問者」という意味の「お客さん」という言葉が「顧客」をさすのに用いられることに気がついた。

　次の日の朝、駅のプラットフォームで電車を待っていた時、駅員が乗客のひとりに「お客さん」と呼びかけるのを聞いた。なるほど、乗客も「お客さん」なのだなと思った。

Mr. Lerner wondered why the Japanese call a customer or passenger by the same name as a visitor; the latter does not involve payment while the former does. Then Sensee said that they all belong to the same category—someone who temporarily stays in the group. A customer is, in a sense, a visitor to a store and a passenger is a visitor to the railway company.

*   *   *

An *okyakusan* stays inside the group only for a limited time, and this fact results in how he is treated. Since he is not a member of the group in the strict sense, he is treated differently from the members. He is usually treated kindly and generously: the host will feed him with the best food he has; the *okyakusan* is asked to sit in the best seat and to take a bath first, etc. But he cannot fully participate in the activities of the group members. An *okyakusan* usually does not help wash the dishes after dinner, for instance; even if he offers to, the hostess will not let him.

Foreigners staying in Japan often feel that they are not accepted in Japanese groups and attribute this to their being foreigners. But Japanese themselves have a difficult time being accepted into a new group. In fact, an *okyakusan* is treated as such regardless of whether he is Japanese or a foreigner. Foreigners are treated differently mainly because they are *okyakusan* in Japanese society. This means that foreigners can be accepted as members of the group when they stop being regarded as *okyakusan*. That takes a long time and requires the satisfaction of various conditions depending on the nature of the group they want to get into. Thinking about a Japanese visitor hesitating at the entrance before stepping into a house may help you understand how an *okyakusan* is supposed to behave. The host will ask him to come into the house by saying

日本では顧客も乗客も、訪問者をさすのと同じ言葉で呼ぶのはなぜであろう、と Mr. Lerner は思った。訪問者は金と関係ないが、顧客や乗客は金を支払うものだ。先生の話では、その集団に一時的に属する、という意味で、すべて同じ範疇に入るということだった。顧客はある意味では店の訪問者であり、乗客は鉄道会社の訪問者というわけだというのである……。

＊　　　　　＊　　　　　＊

「お客さん」はその集団の中に限られた時間だけ滞在する者で、その扱いもこの事実からきている。お客さんは厳密な意味ではその集団の一員ではないから、集団員とは異なった扱いを受ける。通常その扱いは親切かつ寛大である。主人は最も上等の食べ物を提供する。最上の席にすわらせ、風呂にはまっさきに入らせる等々。しかし、お客さんは、その集団の成員の活動に完全に参加することはできない。大抵の場合、食事のあと片づけもしない。やりたいと申し出ても、主婦は許さない。

日本に滞在する外国人は、自分たちはしばしば日本人の集団に受け入れられていないと感じ、それは自分たちが外国人だからだと考える。しかし、日本人自身も、新しい集団に受け入れられる時には困難を体験するのであって、実はお客さんとしての待遇には、日本人も外国人も違いはないのである。

外国人が特別扱いを受けるのは、日本の社会におけるお客さんだからで、お客さんと見なされなくなれば、その集団の一員となるわけである。そのためには長い時間がかかるし、入りたいと思う集団の性格によって、さまざまな条件を満たすことが必要である。

日本人が人を訪問する時、家の中に入る前に玄関で躊躇する様子を考えれば、お客さんがいかなる行動を期待されているか、理解しやすくなるであろう。主人は、

Doozo oagari-kudasai.
(Please come in.)

and the visitor will say

Demo, ojama-deshoo-kara . . .
(But I'd be disturbing you . . .)

After this is repeated a couple of times, the visitor will decide to "disturb" the family members. This is not a mere ceremony; it has to be done in order to show the *okyakusan*'s sincere respect for the group and to express his fear that he may disturb, rather than benefit, the group members by joining them.

(April 23, 1978)

Yoso
よそ
Other places

A few days ago Mr. Lerner heard Mr. Takada talking over the phone with someone who was probably from some other company. It seemed that he was explaining the reason why he had to refuse that person's request. Mr. Lerner heard him say

Yoso-wa soo-kamo shiremasen-ga . . .
(That may be so in other companies, but . . .)

どうぞおあがりください

とすすめるが、訪問者は、

でも、おじゃまでしょうから……

とためらう。こうしたことが1、2度繰り返されてから、訪問者は「おじゃま」することを決意する。これは単なる儀礼ではない。その集団に対する心からの敬意を示すと同時に、自分が加わることによって、その集団を益するのでなくじゃまするのではないかという懸念を表明するために、必要なことなのである。

（1978.4.23）

よそ

Other places

　2、3日前、Mr. Takada がだれか他社の人らしい相手と電話で話しているのが聞こえてきた。その人の頼みを断った理由を説明しているらしかったが、

よそはそうかもしれませんが……

と言っているのが聞こえた。
　「よそ」というのはどういう意味か、Mr. Lerner は知りたいと思った。辞書を

Mr. Lerner wanted to know the meaning of the word *yoso*; the dictionary says that it means "another place" or "strange place," so he guessed that Mr. Takada had used this word to mean "other companies." He wondered if this applies to places other than companies.

*   *   *

Yoso is used to refer to places other than one's own; *yoso-no kaisha* means "other companies" and *yoso-no gakkoo* "other schools" as opposed to one's own company or school. In this sense *yoso-no* is different from *hoka-no* (other). The antonym for *yoso-no kaisha* is *uchi-no kaisha* as in

> *Yoso-no kaisha-wa soo-kamo shiremasen-ga, uchi-no kaisha-wa chigaimasu.*
>
> (That may be so in other companies, but not in our company.)

And *kaisha* in *yoso-no kaisha* and *uchi-no kaisha* can be left out when it is understood as in Mr. Takada's speech above, *Yoso-wa soo-kamo shiremasen-ga . . .*

Thus when one uses the word *yoso*, one is conscious of his own group as contrasted with others. A school principal may say to his students who demand to be given as much freedom as students of other schools

> *Uchi-no gakkoo-wa yoso-towa chigau-n-da.*
>
> (Our school is different from others.)

Yoso-no hito or *yoso-mono* means "a stranger" who has nothing to do with the speaker and the members of his group as in

> *Yoso-mono-niwa wakaranai.*
>
> (An outsider wouldn't understand us.)

The adjective *yoso-yoso-shii* (lit., like another place) describes a person

引いてみると、「ほかのところ」「知らないところ」とあったので、Mr. Takada の言った「よそ」は「他社」の意味であろうと推測したが、他社以外の場所にも使えるのかなと思った……。

＊　　　　　＊　　　　　＊

「よそ」は自分のところ以外の場所をさす。「よその会社」は「ほかの会社」であり、「よその学校」は「ほかの学校」であるが、それぞれ自分の会社や学校に対するもので、その点では「よその」と「ほかの」は同じではない。「よその会社」に対するものは「うちの会社」であって、

うちの会社はそうかもしれませんが、うちの会社は違います

のように用いる。そして、「よその会社」「うちの会社」の「会社」は自明の場合には省いて、Mr. Takada が言ったように「よそは知りませんが……」のように使う。

このように、「よそ」を用いる時は、他と対比された自分のグループを意識する。ほかの学校のように自由にしてほしいという学生に対して、校長が、

うちの学校はよそとは違うんだ

と答える場合もあろう。

「よその人」「よそ者」は、話し手やその集団と関係のない他人の意味で、

よそ者にはわからない

のように使われる。

「よそよそしい」という形容詞は、同じ集団に属していないかのようにふるまうことについて用いられる。「よそいき（よそゆき）」は、文字通りには「よそへ行く時の」の意味で、通常は衣服に用いるが、比喩的に顔つき、話しかた、ふるまいなどにも用いられる。子供のころ、「よそいき」を着なさいと言われた時の

behaving as if not belonging to the same group. *Yoso-yuki* or *yoso-iki* which literally means "going to some other place" usually refers to clothing, but figuratively it can refer to one's look, speech or behavior. Most people remember how excited they were to wear *yoso-iki* clothes when they were children; they also recall that they had to behave better when they wore *yoso-iki*. This is not limited to children. Most Japanese think that they have to behave differently when they leave their home and go to *yoso*.

(January 13, 1980)

Ton ton

トン トン

Knocking

During the lunch hour yesterday, someone started talking about the sound one makes when walking. He said that he could tell who was going by without looking and just listening to the sound. Mr. Lerner learned various onomatopoeic expressions such as *suta suta* (a quick, light sound), *peta peta* (a slapping sound), and *dosun dosun* (a heavy, thumping sound). Then Miss Yoshida said that she could tell when Mr. Lerner was knocking on the door even when she was inside the room. The secret was very simple; while other people knocked two times as in

Ton, ton.

Mr. Lerner knocked three times as

心のときめきを思い出す人も多いであろう。「よそいき」を着た時は、お行儀もよくしなさいと言われたものだ。これは子供に限ったことではない。家を出てよそへ行く時は行動も改めるものだと、大抵の日本人は考えている。

(1980.1.13)

トントン

Knocking

　昨日の昼食どき、だれかが人の歩く時の足音の話を始めた。足音を聞けば、姿を見なくてもだれだかわかるとその人は言う。そして足音を形容するさまざまな擬音語——スタスタ、ペタペタ、ドスンドスンなど——が話題にのぼった。すると Miss Yoshida が、室内にいても Mr. Lerner のノックの音がわかると言った。その秘密は簡単で、ほかの人が2度、

　　トン、トン

とたたくのに、Mr. Lerner は3度、

　　トントントン

とたたくのだそうである。Mr. Lerner は自分のノックの音が日本人の音と違うな

97

Ton ton ton.

He had never realized that he knocked differently from the Japanese, and wondered what impression his knocking made on them.

*   *   *

There seems to be no definite pattern among foreigners about how many times they knock on the door at one time, although knocking three times seems to be frequent among Westerners. On the other hand, Japanese usually knock two times; knocking three times or more implies an emergency. When a Japanese is in a room and hears the door knocked on three times or more in succession, he fears that something unusual has happened and hurries to the door. In a sense, foreigners who knock three times can be unintentionally frightening the Japanese around them.

There are several set expressions in Japanese composed of two repeated parts. The opening expression used on the phone is *moshi-moshi* (hello); probably because of this the Japanese often say "Hello, hello" when speaking English, even when they are not particularly anxious or impatient. Another expression is *bai bai,* derived from the English "bye"; in this case too, the Japanese always say *bai bai.*

(April 12, 1981)

どとは考えてもみなかったが、自分のたたきかたは日本人にどんな印象を与えるのだろうと思った……。

＊　　　　　＊　　　　　＊

　外国人がドアをノックする時続けて何回たたくか、別に決まった形があるわけではないが、欧米人の場合は３回ノックすることが多いようである。それに対して日本人のノックは大抵２回であって、３回以上続けてたたくと非常事態を感じさせる。日本人が室内にいて、３回以上続けざまにノックするのを聞くと、何か大変なことが起こったのではないかと思って急いで戸口へかけつける。ある意味では、３回ノックする外国人は、そのつもりはなくても周囲の日本人をおびやかしている場合があり得る。

　日本語には、２回同じ音を繰り返した表現がいくつかある。電話口での「もしもし」もそうである。たぶんこれが原因と思われるが、日本人が英語を話すとき、別に不安や焦慮を感じていなくても、"Hello, hello." と繰り返すことがよくある。もうひとつの例は「バイバイ」である。英語の "bye" から来ているが、この場合も日本人は必ず「バイバイ」と繰り返して言う。

（1981.4.12）

Soo-desu-ne. Soo-desu-yo.
そうですね。そうですよ。
That's right. That's right.

Mr. Lerner got tired of saying *Soo-desu-ne* all the time to show agreement. Since *Soo-desu-yo* seemed to mean the same thing, he thought he would try using it instead.

One morning in front of the station, he met Mr. Okada, who said with a smile, *Hayai-desu-ne* (You're early).

Instead of saying *Soo-desu-ne*, Mr. Lerner said *Soo-desu-yo*. Mr. Okada looked a little surprised and then said, *Samuku narimashita-ne* (It has become cold). Since Mr. Lerner wanted to strongly emphasize his agreement, he said loudly,

Ee, soo-desu-yo.

Mr. Okada did not talk much during the ride on the train that morning. Mr. Lerner suspected that the shift from *-ne* to *-yo* had produced some bad effect.

*   *   *

There is a great difference between *-yo* and *-ne,* and using *-yo* in the wrong way can be quite damaging to good relations with your Japanese friends and acquaintances.

Ne is used to show your own agreement and your expectation that the listener will agree with you. Thus greetings which refer to the weather

そうですね。そうですよ。

That's right. That's right.

　Mr. Lerner は、賛意を表すのにいつも「そうですね」ばかり言うことにあきてしまい、「そうですよ」も同じ意味のようだから、こっちを使ってみようと思い立った。

　ある朝、駅前でいっしょになった Mr. Okada がにこにこしながら「早いですね」と言ったので、「そうですね」と言う代わりに「ソウデスヨ」と言ってみた。Mr. Okada はちょっと驚いた様子だったが、「寒くなりましたね」と続けた。Mr. Lerner は大いに共感を示したいと思ったので、声を高くして、

　　エエ、ソウデスヨ

と言った。

　その日は電車に乗ってからも、Mr. Okada はあまり物を言わなかった。「ね」から「よ」に変えたのはまずかったのかなと Mr. Lerner は気になった……。

＊　　　　　＊　　　　　＊

　「よ」と「ね」の間には大きな違いがあり、「よ」を誤って用いると、日本人の友人や知人との関係を損なう恐れもある。

　「ね」は話し手の賛同と、聞き手の賛同への期待を示す。天候についてのあいさつなどは、相手との一体感をかもし出すためのものであるから、常に「ね」で終わるのは当然のことである。

　それに対して、「よ」のほうは、相手の考えはどうであろうと、話し手の判断

always end in *-ne* because they are exchanged to create a feeling of oneness between two people.

On the other hand, *-yo* is used to emphatically state your own judgment, regardless of what the listener might think. It is often used to tell someone information he should know or to tell him what he should do. Mothers say *Moo hachiji desu-yo* (It's already eight o'clock!) or *Moo osoi-desu-yo* (It's getting late!) to urge their children to hurry. Thus you have to be careful not to overuse *yo*; otherwise you might impress others as an aggressive, patronizing speaker.

However *-yo* should be used to encourage the listener by denying his uneasiness or his lack of confidence. *Sonna koto-wa arimasen-yo* (That's not so) is the appropriate answer to such statements as "I'm poor at this," or "I don't have any talent for this." Doctors say *Daijoobu-desu-yo* (Don't worry) to a nervous patient before his surgical operation. In this usage also, *-yo* should not be used too much when speaking to your superiors.

No other words are so short and yet so significant as *-ne* and *-yo*.

Ki-o tsukenakucha ikemasen-ne.

(We should be careful, shouldn't we?)

Ki-o tsukenakucha ikemasen-yo.

(You should be careful, I tell you.)

(November 7, 1976)

を強調して示すのに用いられる。当然相手が知っているべきことや、相手のなすべきことを告げる時に「よ」が用いられる。母親が子供をせかす時は「もう8時ですよ」とか「もうおそいですよ」と言う。「よ」の使いすぎに注意しないと、攻撃的に聞こえたり、いばっている印象を与えたりする恐れがある。

　ただし、相手の不安や自信の欠如を否定して、相手を勇気づけたりする時は、「よ」が適当である。「わたしはへただから」とか「才能がないので」というような弱気の発言には、「そんなことはありませんよ」と言うのが適切となる。手術を前にして不安になっている患者に対して、医者は「大丈夫ですよ」と言う。ただ、このような場合でも、目上の人に対しては多用しないことである。

　短い語であるが「ね」「よ」のもつ力には測り知れないものがある。「気をつけなくちゃいけませんね」は "We should be careful, shouldn't we?" に、「気をつけなくちゃいけませんよ」は "You should be careful, I tell you." に当たる。

（1976.11.7）

Nomitai-desu-ka
のみたいですか
Do you want to drink it?

Professor Takahashi, who lived a few doors away, visited Mr. Ernest Lerner one afternoon. Mr. Lerner wanted to serve him a cup of tea, and asked, meaning "Would you like to have some tea?":

Ocha-o nomitai-desu-ka.

(Do you want to drink some tea?)

Prof. Takahashi said *Iie* (No) rather bluntly.

Since his guest was much older, Mr. Lerner thought he should have spoken more politely, and he tried asking the same question again using very polite phrasing.

Ocha-o onomi-ni naritai-desu-ka.

To this painstaking courtesy, Prof. Takahashi still did not respond too warmly, and the conversation after that did not go smoothly. It seemed as if Mr. Lerner had made his offer in the wrong way.

*　　　　*　　　　*

Some people will say Mr. Lerner should have said,

Ocha-demo ikaga-desu-ka.

(Would you care for a cup of tea?)

Some people will say he should have served tea without asking. In any case, the trouble seems to be with the word *nomitai*.

飲みたいですか

Do you want to drink it?

　ある日の午後、近所に住む Professor Takahashi が訪ねてきた。Mr. Lerner はお茶を出そうかと思い、"Would you like to have some tea?" のつもりで、

　　　オ茶ヲ飲ミタイデスカ

とたずねた。

　Prof. Takahashi はやや無愛想に「いいえ」と言った。

　かなり年配のお客なのだから、もっと丁寧な言いかたをすべきだったと反省した Mr. Lerner は、言葉づかいを改めて、

　　　オ茶ヲオ飲ミニナリタイデスカ

とやってみた。

　こうした苦心も Prof. Takahashi には通じなかったようで、会話もあまりはずまなかった。どうやら Mr. Lerner のお茶のすすめかたはまずかったらしい……。

＊　　　　　　＊　　　　　　＊

　この場合、

　　　お茶でもいかがですか

とすべきだったと思う人もあるだろう。また、何も聞かずにお茶を出してしまえばよかったのだと言う人もあろう。いずれにしても、問題は「飲ミタイ」という

Tai, the last part of *nomitai*, means "want to." It is not used, however, to ask someone else's wish when politeness is required. Japanese feel that a person's wish is purely a private matter, and that it is improper, not only impolite, to ask about it directly.

To be polite, in any language, there are things one can talk about and things one shouldn't; asking someone else's wish is considered to be the latter in Japan.

It is quite different among Westerners, especially English-speaking people. Some Westerners complain that Japanese often go ahead and put sugar and cream in the tea or coffee of their guests without first asking. Some Japanese, on the other hand, feel embarrassed when asked exactly in what way they would like their beverage to be prepared.

To ask or not to ask, that seems to be the question, but the question can be resolved if the people on both sides are prepared for either way of politeness.

(August 15, 1976)

Wakarimashita-ka
わかりましたか
Did you understand?

A few weeks ago Mr. Lerner was explaining his proposal in Japanese to several people including the director, Mr. Mori, and Mr. Takada. When he had finished explaining the first part, he felt uncertain about whether or

言葉にあるようである。

「たい」という助動詞は希求を表すが、敬意表現を要求される場合には、他者の希求には用いられない。人の願いは全く個人的なもので、他人の願いを直接たずねるのは、礼にはずれるばかりでなく、妥当性を欠く、と日本人は感じている。

どの言語でも、口にすべきこととしてはならぬことがあるが、他者の欲求を口にすることは、日本では慎むべきこととされている。

欧米の場合、特に英語国民の場合は全く逆である。欧米人の中には、日本では客の好みを聞かずに、紅茶やコーヒーに砂糖やクリームを入れてしまうと言って、怒る人もいる。日本人のほうは逆に、いちいち飲み物についての指定を要求されるとまごついてしまう。

希望を聞くか聞かないか、それは問題であるが、両者とも、互いの敬意表現の形式に理解をもつことが、問題の解決につながるであろう。

（1976.8.15）

わかりましたか

Did you understand?

2、3週間前のこと、Mr. Lerner は社長の Mr. Mori や Mr. Takada ら数人の人を前に、日本語で企画説明を行った。最初の部分の説明を終わった時、理解してもらえたかどうか不安だったので、

not his listeners had understood him, so he asked

Wakarimashita-ka.
(Did you understand?)

Mr. Takada smiled in the way that he did when he noticed one of Mr. Lerner's mistakes in Japanese, and said *Ee, wakarimashita*, but Mr. Mori remained silent, looking rather displeased. Mr. Lerner thought that he had not been polite enough, so he said *owakari-ni narimashita-ka*, choosing a more polite phrasing, but it didn't seem to work.

*   *   *

It is natural for the speaker to want to make sure that the listener has understood him properly; this is especially true when the speaker is using a foreign language. In English, the speaker will use such expressions as "Did you understand?" "Did you get me?" "I hope you understood," or "I hope my explanation has been clear so far," depending on the situation.

In Japanese also, there are a variety of expressions and you have to be careful to choose the right one when you want to be polite. *Wakarimashita-ka* or *Wakarimasu-ka* (Do you understand?) should be avoided when talking to one's superiors. It would sound as if you were talking to a younger person or to a student. This is because the verb *wakaru* implies a person's mental ability; it sounds impolite to question someone's ability to understand even if the speaker means that his own explanation was not lucid enough. Using polite phrasing such as *Owakari-ni narimashita-ka* would make little difference.

Instead, in polite speech, the speaker has to resort to various indirect expressions to check the listener's understanding.

Yoroshii-deshoo-ka.
(Is it all right?)

　　　ワカリマシタカ

ときいた。

　Mr. Takada は、Mr. Lerner がまずい日本語を使った時に示す例の微笑を浮かべて、「ええ、わかりました」と言った。だが Mr. Mori はものも言わず、不機嫌な顔をしていた。言いかたがあまり丁寧でなかったのだと思った Mr. Lerner は、言葉づかいを改めて、

　　　オワカリニナリマシタカ

と言い直したが、これも功を奏さなかった……。

＊　　　　　＊　　　　　＊

　話し手としては、自分の言ったことが正しく伝わったかどうか、確認したいと思うのは当然であるし、外国語で話す場合にはなおさらそうである。英語では場合に応じて、「理解したか」「理解したと思うが」「はっきり説明できたと思うが」という意味の表現をよく使う。

　日本語にもいくつかの表現があり、丁寧な話しかたをする時には、適切なものを選ぶように注意する。「わかりましたか」「わかりますか」は、目上の人に向かって使うべきではない。これでは年下の者や学生に話しているような印象を与えてしまう。これは「わかる」という動詞は人の知的能力に関係をもつからで、たとえ自分の説明が明確でないからという意味であっても、相手の理解能力を疑うような言いかたをするのは失礼なのである。言葉だけ丁重にして、「おわかりになりましたか」と言っても、失礼さに変わりはない。

　丁寧な話しかたでは、さまざまな間接的な表現によって、聞き手の理解を確かめなければならない。

　　　よろしいでしょうか

or

Tsugi-e itte-mo yoroshii-deshoo-ka.

(Is it all right to go on to the next part?)

is often used for this purpose.

Another method is to stimulate the listener's reaction by throwing out some dangling statement such as *Soo yuu wake-na-n-desu-ga* . . . (Such is the situation and . . .) or *Soo yuu koto-de* . . . (Such is the fact and . . .). Then the listener will usually say that he has understood so far and wants to hear more. The idea is that the speaker should ask the listener if it is all right to go on rather than trying to directly check the listener's understanding.

(July 9, 1978)

Kore, agemasu
これ、あげます
I'll give this to you

When Mr. Lerner went to Kyoto last week, he bought a package of green tea. He wanted to give it to Mr. Mori, the director of the company, who likes good tea. While handing the package to Mr. Mori, he said

Kore, tsumaranai mono-desu-ga, agemasu.

(This is very little, —lit., This is a trifling thing,—but I'll give it to you.)

Mr. Mori thanked him, but Mr. Lerner felt something was wrong with his Japanese, so he corrected himself and said

次に行ってもよろしいでしょうか

などがよく用いられる。

　もうひとつの方法は、聞き手の反応を引き出すために、「そういうわけなんですが……」とか「そういうことで……」のような、不確定な言いかたをしてみることである。それを聞くと聞き手は、そこまではわかったから次をどうぞ、と答えるのが普通である。

　大切なのは、聞き手が理解したかを直接問うのでなく、次へ進んでもよいかとたずねるという態度である。

（1978.7.9）

これ、あげます

I'll give this to you

　先週京都へ行った時、Mr. Lerner は一包みの緑茶を買った。お茶の味にやかましい社長の Mr. Mori に贈りたいと思ったのである。社長に手渡しながら、

　　　コレ、ツマラナイモノデスガ、アゲマス

と言った。Mr. Mori はお礼を言ったが、Mr. Lerner はどうも日本語がまずかったらしいと感じたので、

　　　コレ、サシアゲマス

と言い直した。「さしあげる」のほうが「あげる」より謙譲の印象を持つと習っ

Kore, sashiagemasu.

(I'll give this to you.)

because he had learned that *sashiageru* is more humble than *ageru*. But from Mr. Mori's look, this expression did not seem quite appropriate either.

*   *   *

Dictionaries give several words corresponding to the English "give" such as *yaru*, *ageru*, and *sashiageru*. Grammar books explain that *sashiageru* is the most polite of those three and should be used when giving something to your superior. But when one actually gives something in a social situation, *sashiageru* is not necessarily the most appropriate expression.

It is not quite appropriate to use any word directly meaning "to give" in social situations, just as *kau* (to buy) is not usually used when buying things. A customer says *Sore, kudasai* (Please give it to me) or *Sore, moraimashoo* (I'll take it) rather than saying *Sore, kaimasu* (I'll buy it).

To be polite when giving a present, one chooses from different expressions such as:

Yoroshikattara meshiagatte-kudasai.

(Please eat it if it's all right.)

Yoroshikattara otsukai-kudasai.

(Please use it if it's all right.)

Doozo oosame-kudasai.

(Please accept it.)

Or, one chooses to sound apologetic as in

Tsumaranai mono-desu-ga . . .

(This is very little, but . . .)

ていたからである。しかし Mr. Mori の顔つきから見ると、この表現も極めて適切とは言えなかったらしい……。

＊　　　　　＊　　　　　＊

辞書を見ると英語の "give" に当たる言葉として、「やる、あげる、さしあげる」などがあげてある。文法書には、この 3 語のうちで「さしあげる」が最も丁寧で、目上の人に物を贈る時に用いられると書いてある。しかし、実際に社会的な場面で物を贈る時には、「さしあげる」が必ずしも最も適切な表現であるとは限らない。

社会的な場面では、"to give" に直接対応する言葉を使うのは、必ずしも適切ではない。物を買う時にも「買う」という語が普通用いられないのと同じである。客は「それ、下さい」とか「それ、もらいましょう」とは言うが、「それ、買います」とは普通言わない。

贈り物を渡す時の丁寧な表現としては、全く別の形を用いて、

　　よろしかったら召しあがってください
　　よろしかったらお使いください
　　どうぞお納めください

などと言う。

あるいは、非礼を詫びるような形をとって、

　　つまらないものですが……
　　ほんの一口ですが……

のような言いかたをする。このような「詫び」に似た表現のあとには「どうぞ」とか「どうぞ召しあがってください」などが、よく省かれる。省かないで言うとしても、声を弱めて言うのが普通である。

（1979.10.14）

Honno hitokuchi-desu-ga . . .

(This is very little [lit., It's just one mouthful], but . . .)

After these apologetic remarks, such expressions as *Doozo* (Please) or *Doozo meshiagatte-kudasai* are often left out. And even when they are said, they're pronounced rather softly.

(October 14, 1979)

Chotto . . .
ちょっと…
A little bit . . .

A few weeks ago Mr. Lerner and Miss Yoshida were having coffee during their break at work, when Mr. Takada came and asked them if they could come to his house on the next Saturday. Mr. Lerner said he would come, but Miss Yoshida said,

Sono hi-wa chotto . . .

(lit., That day is a little bit . . .)

Then Mr. Takada immediately said he hoped she could come next time, without waiting for her to complete the sentence. Later he explained to Mr. Lerner that *chotto* stood for *Chotto tsugoo-ga warui-n-desu* (it's little bit inconvenient for me).

But yesterday afternoon Miss Yoshida came to Mr. Lerner and said,

ちょっと…

A little bit . . .

　2、3週間前、会社の休み時間に Mr. Lerner と Miss Yoshida がコーヒーを飲んでいると、Mr. Takada が来て、次の土曜日に家へ遊びに来ないかと言った。Mr. Lerner は行くと言ったが、Miss Yoshida は、

　　その日はちょっと……

と言った。

　すると Mr. Takada はすぐ、彼女が文を終わるのを待ちもせず、じゃ今度来てねと言った。そしてあとで Mr. Lerner に、「ちょっと」というのは「ちょっと都合が悪いんです」の意味だと説明した。

　しかし昨日の午後、Miss Yoshida が来て、

Anoo, chotto . . .

(lit., Excuse me, a little bit . . .)

It took some time for him to understand that she meant *Chotto onegai-ga aru-n-desu-ga* (Will you do a little favor for me?).

*   *   *

Chotto is used in several different ways in daily conversation. It is used most often in requests and refusals.

When making a request, *chotto* is used to start the sentence as in

Chotto matte-kudasai.

(Please wait a moment.)

Chotto onegai-shimasu.

(Please do me a favor.)

In such sentences *chotto* can be left out, but when it is included, it shows the speaker's reluctance to trouble others so that the sentences sound more reserved and considerate. In doing this, however, it must be said with a hesitant tone and is often preceded by *Anoo* or *Ano*. If *Chotto!* alone is said without a hesitant tone, it sounds rude. (Some people use it when calling to someone they do not know on the street, but it is impolite.)

When refusing, *chotto* is very convenient because it shows the speaker's reluctance. If someone answers your request with

Sore-wa chotto . . .

he means that he cannot do it but is unhappy to tell you so.

Reluctance is also appropriate when giving a negative evaluation. If you show your plan to someone and he says,

Chotto . . .

　　あのう、ちょっと……

と言うではないか。
　これが「ちょっとお願いがあるんですが」の意味であるということが、Mr. Lerner にはなかなかのみこめなかった……。

＊　　　　　　＊　　　　　　＊

　「ちょっと」は日常生活でいくつかの用法を持つ。最もよく用いられるのは、依頼と断りの場面である。
　依頼の場合には文を始めるのに用いられる。

　　ちょっと待ってください
　　ちょっとお願いします

　このような文では、「ちょっと」がなくても意味は通じるが、「ちょっと」が入ると、話し手が、相手に迷惑をかけたくないと思っている気持ちが表れ、遠慮がちな、思いやりのある話しかたになる。しかし、そのためには、ためらいがちな調子で言うことが必要で、またよく「あのう」や「あの」が先に立つ。もし「ちょっと！」とだけはっきりした口調で言うと、ぶしつけな感じになる。（道で知らない人に「ちょっと！」と呼びかける人もあるが、これは失礼である。）
　頼みを断る時にも、「ちょっと」は断りたくない気持ちを表すので都合がよい。何か頼んだ時、相手が、

　　それはちょっと……

と言ったら、希望に添えないがそう言いたくないという意味である。
　否定的な評価を示す場合にも、不本意な気持ちを表したほうが礼儀にかなう。人に企画を見てもらった時、その人が、

　　ちょっと……

It means he has some reservations about it. He can be more specific by saying

Koko-ga chotto . . .

(lit., In this point a little bit . . .)

or

Hiyoo-no ten-de chotto . . .

(lit., In terms of cost, a little bit . . .)

(June 5, 1977)

Dekinai wake-ja arimasen-kedo . . .

できない わけじゃ ありませんけど…

I don't mean to say that I can't but . . .

Yesterday afternoon Mr. Lerner wanted to have some papers ready for the next day. He asked Miss Yoshida if she could type them for him. She looked through the draft and said

Soo-desu-nee . . .

(Well, . . .)

Mr. Lerner couldn't very well force her to do it because he was rather late in getting the draft ready, so he asked her if it was impossible. She said

Dekinai wake-ja arimasen-kedo . . .

(I don't mean to say that I can't but . . .)

と言ったら、賛意を保留するという意味である。特定の理由を示す場合には、

　　ここがちょっと……

とか、

　　費用の点でちょっと……

のように言う。

（1977.6.5）

できないわけじゃありませんけど…

I don't mean to say that I can't but . . .

　昨日の午後、Mr. Lerner は翌日のためにいくつか書類を準備したいと思ったので、Miss Yoshida にタイプを頼みに行った。彼女は原稿に目を通して、

　　そうですねえ……

と言った。Mr. Lerner としては、原稿の仕上がりがおそかったので無理にとは言えない立場にあったから、だめだろうかときいた。Miss Yoshida は、

　　できないわけじゃありませんけど……

と言った。そのあと何か言うのかと思って待ったが、彼女のほうも Mr. Lerner が何か言い出すのを待っているようであった。これはあまりやりたくないのだと

119

Mr. Lerner waited for her to complete her sentence, but it was as if she was waiting for him to say something. He sensed that she didn't want to do it very much, so he offered to do part of the typing himself and she agreed.

*   *   *

The expression . . . *wake-ja arimasen* (lit., the situation isn't that . . .) itself means "I don't mean to say that . . ." *Dekinai wake-ja arimasen-kedo* can be followed by such phrases as *kiree-ni dekinai-kamo shiremasen* (I may not be able to do it neatly) or *zangyoo-shinakereba narimasen* (I'll have to work overtime). But when . . . *wake-ja arimasen* is used with *kedo* or *ga* (but) alone, the speaker is usually implying refusal. Many Japanese find it difficult to say "no" directly to someone's request when they want to refuse it, so they use various expressions in order to avoid saying "no"; . . . *wake-ja arimasen-kedo* is often used as one of these expressions, as in

Dame-da-to yuu wake-ja arimasen-kedo . . .
(I'm not saying no but . . .)
Hantai-suru wake-ja arimasen-ga . . .
(I don't mean to oppose you but . . .)

After these expressions, the speaker waits for the other to say something. In other words, he would rather have the request-maker take back his request on his own accord.

To avoid saying "no" to someone's request, various other expressions are used such as:

Sore-wa chotto . . .
(lit., That is a little . . .)
Sore-wa doo-deshoo-ne.
(I wonder about that.)

いう察しがついたので、一部は自分でタイプをしようと言い、彼女はそれで引き受けた……。

＊　　　　　　＊　　　　　　＊

「～わけじゃありません」は文字通りには「～という状況ではない」という意味であるが、実際には "I don't mean to say that . . ."（～と言うつもりではない）の意味に用いられる。「できないわけじゃありませんけど」のあとには、「きれいにできないかもしれません」とか、「残業しなければなりません」のような表現がくる場合もある。しかし、「～わけじゃありません」に「けど」や「が」がついただけであれば、暗に拒絶を示しているのが普通である。日本人の多くは人に何か頼まれた場合、断りたいと思ってもはっきり "no" とは言いにくいと感じるので、"no" を言わずにすませるために、さまざまな表現に訴える。「～わけじゃありませんけど／が」もこうした場合の表現のひとつで、

> だめだというわけじゃありませんけど……
> 反対するわけじゃありませんが……

のようによく用いられる。
　このような表現のあとでは、話し手は相手が何か言うのを待つ。言いかえれば、依頼した当人が自分から進んで依頼を取り下げるのを望んでいるのである。
　人の依頼を断るのに "no" を言わずにすませる方法として、

> それはちょっと……
> それはどうでしょうねえ
> お引き受けしたいのは山々ですが……

などが用いられる。また「そうですね……」や「それは……」も、ためらいがちで残念そうな口調の場合、暗に否定的な返答であることが示される。

（1979.12.30）

Ohikiuke-shitai-nowa yamayama-desu-ga . . .

(I would like to do it very much but . . .)

Or, *Soo-desu-nee . . .* or *Sore-wa . . .* can imply a negative answer when said with a hesitant, regretful tone.

(December 30, 1979)

Mooshiwake arimasen-ga, anoo . . .
もうしわけ ありませんが、あのう…
I'm very sorry, but . . .

The other day Mr. Lerner and Mr. Takada went to Mr. Okada's office to discuss some business with him. After the discussion was over, Mr. Okada retained them and continued talking. To Mr. Lerner it seemed as if he were going to talk forever, and he felt irritated because he was rather busy that day. But he thought he should wait for Mr. Takada to say something, and suppressed his irritation.

When the talk seemed to have come to an end and there was a slight pause, Mr. Takada said

Mooshiwake arimasen-ga, anoo . . .

(lit., I have no excuse to offer, but I . . .)

Then Mr. Okada quickly changed his tone and apologized for keeping them too long. Mr. Takada thanked him for spending so much time with them, in which Mr. Lerner joined. When the two stood up and were about

申しわけありませんが、あのう…

I'm very sorry, but . . .

　先日、Mr. Lerner は Mr. Takada とともに Mr. Okada の会社へ商談に出向いた。話し合いが終わってからも、Mr. Okada は 2 人を引きとめて話を続けた。Mr. Lerner は、その話が際限なく続きそうなのを見て、忙しい日だったので内心いらいらしたが、Mr. Takada が何か言い出すのを待つべきだろうと考えて、がまんしていた。

　話が一応の区切りに来てちょっととぎれた時、Mr. Takada は、

　　申しわけありませんが、あのう……

と言った。

　すると Mr. Okada はたちまち口調を変え、2 人を引きとめてすまなかったと詫びた。Mr. Takada は長い間ありがとうございましたと礼を述べ、Mr. Lerner もそれに同調した。Mr. Takada はさり気なく、

to leave, Mr. Takada added casually

Mada sukoshi shigoto-ga arimasu-node . . .
(We have a little more work to do, so . . .)

*   *   *

Mr. Lerner was interested in the way Mr. Takada took his leave, so he asked Sensee if this was typically Japanese.

Sensee said it is. It is typically Japanese in many ways. First, Mr. Takada waited patiently until there was a pause that showed the termination of one topic. In discussing business with Japanese, you usually have to be prepared to spend some time before and after the discussion itself.

Second, he just said that he was sorry and didn't say anything about his having to leave. Mr. Lerner would have said something like

Shigoto-ga arimasu-kara kaeranakereba narimasen.
(Since I have some work to do, I have to leave.)

but Mr. Takada didn't say this. And Mr. Okada immediately took the hint and helped the guests get ready to say good-bye.

Very often a Japanese conversation will proceed without the speaker mentioning his desires and the listener makes an effort to understand these unspoken desires. A teacher of Japanese to foreigners will often feel embarrassed when he hears his students say something like

Moo kaeranakereba narimasen.
(I have to go now.)

when leaving. This sentence is grammatically correct and the speaker means well, but actually Japanese do not usually speak so directly in this

まだ少し仕事がありますので……

とつけ加え、2人は立ちあがって出た……。

＊　　　　＊　　　　＊

Mr. Lerner は Mr. Takada の辞去のしかたに興味をもち、これは典型的な日本のやりかたなのかと先生にきいてみた。

先生はそうだと答え、いろいろな意味で典型的だと説明した。まず、ひとつの話題が終わったことを示す休止が出るまで、辛抱強く待ったことだ。日本人と商談をする時は、通常、話し合いの前後にある程度の時間を割く覚悟をしなければならない。

次に、「申しわけありません」と言うだけで、去る必要のあることは言わなかったことである。Mr. Lerner だったら、

　　仕事ガアリマスカラ、帰ラナケレバナリマセン

というようなことを言ったであろうが、Mr. Takada はそれを言わなかった。そして Mr. Okada はその気持ちをすぐに察して、客が別れを告げやすいように振る舞った。

日本語では、話し手は自分の希望を口にせず、それを聞き手が理解しようと努力する、という形で話が進むことが多い。外国人に日本語を教える教師は、学生が去り際に、

　　モウ帰ラナケレバナリマセン

と言うのを聞くと、ちょっと困ったなという気持ちになる。この文は文法的には間違っていないし、話し手に悪気があるわけではない。しかし日本語では実際には、このようにあからさまな言いかたはしないのが普通である。日本人にとっ

kind of situation. To the Japanese ear, this sounds as if the speaker is unnecessarily asserting himself; it can seem either rude or strangely dramatic.

(June 11, 1978)

Guchi-o yuu
ぐちを 言う
To complain

The other day when Mr. Lerner met Mr. Okada after not having seen him for some time, he thought he looked very tired. Mr. Okada said that someone who had been helping him had suddenly left the company so he was quite busy. When Mr. Lerner asked if the company director was not going to find someone else to help him, he said that the director was not very considerate of him. Mr. Lerner felt sorry for him and wondered if there was anything he could do to help him. Then Mr. Okada looked surprised and told him to forget about it, saying

Guchi-o itta dake-desu-kara.

Mr. Lerner understood that this meant "I was only complaining," but he didn't understand what was implied by *guchi-o itta*.

*   *   *

Guchi-o yuu or *guchi-o kobosu* refers to complaining, usually not to the person who has caused the trouble, but to someone who will listen to the

て、こうした話しかたは、必要以上に自己主張をしていると感じられ、粗野にも大げさにもひびくのである。

（1978.6.11）

ぐちを言う

To complain

この間、久しぶりに会った時、Mr. Okada はかなり疲れている様子で、仕事の手助けをしてくれる人が急に会社をやめたので、忙しくなったと言った。社長はだれか代わりに手伝う人を探してくれないのか、と Mr. Lerner がきくと、社長はあまり自分のことを考えてくれないと言った。Mr. Lerner は気の毒になって、何か力になれることはないだろうかとたずねた。すると Mr. Okada はびっくりした顔をして、どうぞそれはもう忘れてほしい、

　　　ぐちを言っただけですから

と言った。

Mr. Lerner にもその意味は理解できたが、「ぐちを言った」という表現にどんな気持ちが込められているのか、わからなかった……。

＊　　　　　＊　　　　　＊

「ぐちを言う」とか「ぐちをこぼす」というのは、通常、その問題を引き起こした人にでなく、だれか話を聞いて同情してくれる人に不満を訴えることを言

speaker and sympathize with him. In other words, when a person says *gu-chi*, he usually doesn't expect the listener to start any action to solve the problem. What counts is the satisfaction obtained by having an outlet for one's dissatisfaction and being comforted by the listener's sympathy.

Sometimes *kobosu* alone can stand for *guchi-o kobosu*, as in

Kyoo-wa Okada-san, daibu koboshite-ikimashita-ne.
(Mr. Okada complained a lot today.)
Okada-san-ni kobosarete komarimashita.
(Mr. Okada complained so much that I was embarrassed. —lit., I was complained by Mr. Okada so much that I was at a loss.)

When people gather and talk together at bars or restaurants after the day's work, they often complain. They will grumble that they are not paid well enough and that they have to work for bosses who lack any kindness or understanding. When they complain about these things over a cup or coffee or a glass of beer, they usually don't expect their listeners to do something about these problems the next day. This is a typical case of *guchi-o yuu* or *guchi-o kobosu*. And the listeners usually listen to their companions' *guchi* with enthusiastic *aizuchi* (reply words) and expressions of their sympathy.

(November 23, 1980)

う。言いかえれば、「ぐち」を言っている時は、問題を解決するための行動を起こすことは聞き手に期待しないのである。要は、不満のはけ口を得て、相手の同情を受けることによって満足を得ることにある。

　時には「ぐちをこぼす」の代わりに「こぼす」だけで足りることもある。たとえば、

　　きょうは岡田さん、だいぶこぼしていましたね
　　岡田さんにこぼされて困りました

のように言う。

　1日の仕事のあとでバーやレストランに集まってしゃべる時、ぐちが出ることが多い。給料が少ないとか、物わかりの悪い上司や冷たい上役のために働かなければならないなどといった不満を言う。1杯のコーヒー、1杯のビールを前にこうした不満を述べる時、聞き手が翌日何らかの解決策を講じるとは期待していないのが普通である。これが「ぐちを言う」「ぐちをこぼす」の典型的な場合である。そして聞き手は通常、熱心な相づちと同情の表明をもって、相手の「ぐち」に耳を傾けるのである。

（1980.11.23）

De, kyoo-wa . . . ?
で、きょうは…？
Well, what can I do for you today?

The other day Mr. Matsumoto came to see Mr. Lerner and Mr. Takada. He obviously came to discuss some business, but he didn't start talking about it immediately; he talked about his favorite baseball player. Mr. Lerner knew that it is customary for many Japanese businessmen to spend some time like this before a discussion, so he waited patiently for him to start discussing business saying *Jitsu-wa . . .* (As a matter of fact . . .). But Mr. Takada didn't wait long. He agreed with Mr. Matsumoto about the player being the best, and before Mr. Matsumoto started to say anything else, he said

De, kyoo-wa . . . ?
(lit., Then, today . . . ?)

with a sustained tone. Then Mr. Matsumoto immediately started discussing business, and the talk was finished in an amazingly short time.

Mr. Lerner was surprised that Japanese businessmen are not always willing to spend a lot of time in preliminary talk, and that they can make it very short if they want to.

*   *   *

It is customary and regarded as good in Japan to spend some time talking leisurely so that good relations between the two people can be established before the business is discussed. But at the same time, it is also true

で、きょうは…？

Well, what can I do for you today?

　先日 Mr. Matsumoto が Mr. Lerner と Mr. Takada の２人を訪ねてきた。何か事務的な話があるに違いないのだが、すぐにはその話をしようとせず、自分の好きな野球選手の話を始めた。日本のビジネスマンは商談の前にこんな話をするものだと聞いていたので、Mr. Lerner は、彼が「実は……」と言って話を切り出すまで、辛抱づよく待つことにした。ところが Mr. Takada は待たなかった。その選手が最強の選手だという Mr. Matsumoto の意見に賛成の意を示すと、他のことを言い出す間を与えず、

　　　で、きょうは……？

と、言葉じりを引きのばすようにして言った。すると Mr. Matsumoto は直ちに商談にとりかかり、話は驚くほど短時間で終わってしまった。

　日本のビジネスマンも、必ずしも前置きの雑談に長時間を費やすのを喜ばず、短く切りあげたいと思えばそれができるのだと知って、Mr. Lerner は意外に思った……。

*　　　*　　　*

　日本では、仕事の話の前に、両者の間によい関係が確立されるよう、のんびりと雑談をするのが習慣でもあり、よしとされてもいる。しかし、同時に、会ってすぐ仕事の話を始める場合のあることも、事実である。こういう場合には、"What can I do for you?" の意味で、

that sometimes people start discussing business very soon after they meet. In such eases people usually say

De, kyoo-wa . . . ?

or

Kyoo-wa nanika . . . ?

(lit., As for today, anything . . . ?)

to mean "What can I do for you?"

These expressions can be taken as abbreviations of longer sentences. After *De, kyoo-wa . . . ?*, *nan-no goyoo-desu-ka* (lit., what business do you have?) or *nanika goyoo-desu-ka* (lit., do you have some business?) is left out. After *Kyoo-wa nanika . . . ?* various things can be meant without being mentioned. They can be *arimashita-ka* (did anything happen?), *tokubetsu-no ohanashi-ga arimasu-ka* (is there something in particular you want to talk about?) or *okomari-no koto-demo arimasu-ka* (do you have anything that troubles you?).

What is important is that these sentences are not completed in polite inquiries. Saying them out loud sounds rather coarse and impolite; *nanika* is enough and nothing more should be said out loud when one has to be polite. Sometimes just *arimasu-ka* is left out as in

Kyoo-wa nanika tokubetsu-no ohanashi-demo . . . ?

In this type of expression, *-demo* is preferred to *-ga*.

(December 10, 1978)

　で、きょうは……？

とか、

　きょうは何か……？

と言う。

　これらの表現は、もっと長い文を縮めたものと考えることができる。「で、きょうは……？」のあとには、「何の御用ですか」とか「何か御用ですか」などが略されている。「きょうは何か……？」のあとにも、さまざまなことが省略されている。「ありましたか」「特別のお話がありますか」あるいは「お困りのことでもありますか」などである。

　大切なことは、丁寧な質問としては、こうした文を終わりまで言わないということである。全文を声に出して言ってしまうのは、粗野であり失礼である。丁寧に話す時は「何か」で十分で、そのあとは声に出さないのである。時には「ありますか」を省略して、

　きょうは何か特別のお話でも……？

と言ったりするが、こうした話しかたでは、「（お話）が」より「（お話）でも」のほうがよいとされる。

（1978.12.10）

Kaeranakereba narimasen
帰らなければ なりません
I must go home

Mr. Lerner was invited to a little party at Miss Yoshida's the other day. Staying for some time and having a good time, he thought it was about time to leave. When Miss Yoshida tried to retain him, he said

Moo kaeranakereba narimasen.

(I must go home now.)

While the two were talking, Mr. Takada also came to the door and said

Boku-mo sorosoro shitsuree-shimasu.

(I'm leaving too, if you don't mind.)

Mr. Lerner then realized that he should have said *Shitsuree-shimasu*, and remembered that Japanese do not usually say *kaeranakereba narimasen* in such situations.

*   *   *

The expression *kaeranakereba narimasen* is not appropriate when taking leave of someone. In daily conversation such shorter forms as *kaeranakucha* or *kaeranakya* are used in place of *kaeranakereba narimasen*. Sometimes . . . *nakereba narimasen* is used in the middle of a sentence, as in *Haisha-ni ikanakereba narimasen-node* . . . (Since I must go to the dentist . . .), but it is not conversational to end a sentence with . . . *nakereba narimasen*.

帰らなければなりません

I must go home

　先日 Mr. Lerner は、Miss Yoshida の家のちょっとしたパーティーに招かれた。しばらく楽しくすごしたあと、もうそろそろ帰ろうかと思ったので、Miss Yoshida が玄関でひきとめるのに対して、

　　モウ帰ラナケレバナリマセン

と言った。そこへ Mr. Takada もやってきて、

　　ぼくもそろそろ失礼します

と言った。

　それを聞いて Mr. Lerner は、自分も「失礼します」と言うべきだったのだと悟った。こういう状況では日本人は普通「帰らなければなりません」とは言わないのだから……。

＊　　　　　　＊　　　　　　＊

　人にいとまごいをする時、「帰らなければなりません」と言うのは適切ではない。日常の話しかたとしては、「帰らなければなりません」と言うよりはもっと短く、「帰らなくちゃ」「帰らなきゃ」が使われる。「～なければなりません」は文の途中で「歯医者に行かなければなりませんので……」のように使うこともあるが、文の終わりを「～なければなりません」で止めるのは会話的ではない。

　「～なければなりません」は、改まった書き言葉的な文の終わりによく使われ

The form ... *nakereba narimasen* is used to end formal, written sentences as in

Kokumin-wa zeekin-o osamenakereba naranai.

(The people must pay taxes.)

Kono daigaku-ni hairu tame-niwa shiken-o ukenakereba narimasen.

(You have to take an examination to enter this college.)

As seen in these two examples, ... *nakereba narimasen* is used to state one's duty or requirements; therefore it is not appropriate for referring to what one wants to do for one's own good or convenience. Saying *Hachiji-made-ni kaeranakereba narimasen-node* ... would be all right if the purpose of going home before eight is doing one's work, but it would be strange if the purpose is watching one's favorite situation comedy.

Thus when one is taking his leave from his host's house, one usually avoids using ... *nakereba naranai* and chooses such expressions as

Shitsuree-shimasu.

(lit., I'm going to be rude.)

or

Oitoma-shimasu.

(I'm taking my leave.)

(December 2, 1980)

る。たとえば、

> 国民は税金を納めなければならない
> この大学に入るためには試験を受けなければなりません

のように用いられる。

　この2例にあるように、「～なければなりません」は、人の義務や責任を述べるのに用いられる。したがって、自分の利益や都合のためにやりたいと思うことについて使うのは、適切な用法とは言えない。「8時までに帰らなければなりませんので……」というのは、8時までに帰る目的が仕事であればよいが、テレビで好きな喜劇を見るためであったら、奇異な印象を与えるであろう。

　したがって、主人のもとを辞去する時、客は「～なければならない」を避けて、

> 失礼します

とか、

> おいとまします

と言うのが普通である。

（1980.11.2）

Chapter 3

Consideration
toward Others

相手に対する配慮

There are numerous expressions employed to show consideration toward others; here we collected common expressions of apology such as *Gomen-nasai*, *Warui-desu-ne*, and expressions to show sympathy toward others. Such expressions work to make human relations smoother—*Osaki-ni* used when you leaving the work place before others; *Konna jikan-ni sumimasen*, *Oisogashii tokoro-o* . . . when taking someone's time. Foreigner also find *Taihen-desu-ne* (That's tough) to be very useful in showing warm feelings. Humans have to work hard to make a living, but it is important to express sympathy for others' hardships as well.

Otsukaresama-deshita is another good expression of sympathy. Of course there are also appropriate responses to such expressions of sympathy: *Taishita koto-wa arimasen* (It's nothing), *Okagesama-de* (Thanks to you), and *Tasukarimashita* (You helped me).

And a sentence-ending *kedo* or *kara* in such sentences as *Ocha-ga hairimashita-kedo*, or *Ato-de kekkoo-desu-kara* is used to express consideration toward the other, rather than simply being a sign of clumsy speech.

　相手に対する配慮を示す表現は数多くあるが、ここでは特に、一般に使われる「ごめんなさい」「わるいですね」のような詫びの表現から、相手に対するいたわりや配慮を示すものを取り上げた。相手より先に場を去るときの「お先に」や、「こんな時間にすみません」「お忙しいところを……」のような配慮表現は人間関係をなめらかにするのに必要なものである。また「大変ですね」は、多くの外国人からあたたかい共感の表現として好評を得ているものである。人間はそれぞれ生活のために努力しているが、それを当然と見ず相手の苦労に同情を示すことによって、よき人間関係を結びたいと願うことに注目したい。

　また、「おつかれさまでした」は、相手に対するいたわりの表現として外国人の間で好評であるが、配慮表現に対する受け答えも当然考察すべき問題である。「大したことはありません」「おかげさまで」「助かりました」など、日本人社会にとけこみたいと願っている人に知りたかったと感謝された表現の一つである。

　なお、「お茶がはいりましたけど」「あとでけっこうですから」のような、誘いや依頼の文の文末に使われる「けど」「から」に含まれる相手への配慮は、ただなんとなく文を言い切らない優柔不断な話し方であるなどと誤解されないように、ぜひ外国人に正しく理解してもらいたいことである。

Osaki-ni

お先に

Excuse me

Mr. Lerner was invited to a little party at Miss Yoshida's last Saturday, and had a very good time. Mr. Takada was also invited, but he left early, saying that he had to take care of his sick wife. When he was leaving he said

Osaki-ni shitsuree-shimasu.

(lit., I'm going to be rude and leave before you.)

Mr. Lerner remembered that people usually say *Osaki-ni* when leaving the office before others; he had thought that it had to be said because the speaker was leaving when others had to work. He wondered why it has to be said when leaving a party, too. The one leaving early is going to miss the fun, and why does he have to apologize for it? Is it because his absence is going to affect the other people's fun?

*　　　　　*　　　　　*

Osaki-ni by itself can mean either "before you" or "after you." When one says *Doozo osaki-ni* to someone at the entrance of a building or room, for example, it means "Please go ahead" or "After you." In this case, *doozo* is usually added either before or after the phrase.

On the other hand, when one says *Osaki-ni* before doing something, like leaving or helping oneself to food or entering the bath, he means

お先に

Excuse me

　先週の土曜日、Miss Yoshida の家でちょっとしたパーティーがあり、Mr. Lerner も招かれていって、楽しいひとときをすごした。Mr. Takada も来ていたが、女房が病気だからと言って先に帰った。そして帰る時、

　　　お先に失礼します

と言って出ていった。

　「お先に」というのは普通、会社を先に出る時に言うもので、ほかの人が働いているのに帰ってしまうから言うのだ、と Mr. Lerner は理解していた。パーティーから出ていく時にもそう言うのはなぜだろう。先に出る人はそれだけ楽しみを損するわけなのに、なぜ詫びなければいけないのか。自分がいなくなるとほかの人が楽しくなくなるからだろうか……。

＊　　　　＊　　　　＊

　「お先に」自体は「お先にわたしがします」（before you）とも、「お先にどうぞ」（after you）ともとれる。建物や部屋の入口で「どうぞお先に」と言えば、「お先にどうぞお入りください」の意味になる。この場合には、「お先に」の前かあとに「どうぞ」を加えるのが普通である。

　他方、何かをする前、すなわち部屋を出る時、何か食べ始める時、ふろに入る時などの前に「お先に」と言うと、「失礼します」（Excuse me）、つまり「失礼してお先に始めます」の意味になる。この場合には「失礼します」と口に出して言うこともあり、言葉を言わずにすませてしまうこともある。

"Excuse me" or "Excuse me for going ahead of you." In this case *shitsuree-shimasu* is either said verbally or understood after the phrase.

If one belongs to the group, it is appropriate to say *Osaki-ni* or *Osaki-ni shitsuree-shimasu* when leaving the others, whether they may be working or having fun. Saying *Kaerimasu* (I'm going home) or *Ikanakereba nari-masen* (I must go) does not sound appropriate in social situations.

This expression is said not only to one's superiors but also to one's equals or to younger members of the group. The underlying idea for this is that a member of a group is supposed to feel guilty in breaking away from the others and by doing so affecting the unity of the group. It seems that many Japanese regard it as important for a group member to be together with the others, not only emotionally but also physically, both in work and in fun.

(February 15, 1981)

Ocha-ga hairimashita-kedo . . .
お茶が はいりましたけど…
The tea is ready, but . . .

A few weeks ago while Mr. Lerner was working at the office, Miss Yoshida came in and asked him to come over to the tea table saying

Ocha-ga hairimashita-kara . . .
(lit., Because the tea is ready, . . .)

Mr. Lerner understood that she wanted him to come for his tea, although

　人が何らかの集団に属している場合、仕事にせよ遊びにせよそこを離れる時は、「お先に」「お先に失礼します」と言うのが礼儀である。「帰ります」とか「行かなければなりません」と言うのは、人づきあいの場では適切ではない。

　この表現は目上の人ばかりでなく、同輩や年下の者に対しても用いる。この習慣の底には、集団の成員は、集団を離れ、そのために集団の団結を損なうことに、罪の意識をもつべきだという考えがある。多くの日本人にとって集団の成員は、仕事の場でも遊びの場でも、心情的にも身体的にも、いっしょにいることが大切なことだとされているようである。

（1981.2.15）

お茶がはいりましたけど…

The tea is ready, but . . .

　2週間ほど前、Mr. Lerner が会社で仕事をしているところへ、Miss Yoshida がやってきて、

　　お茶がはいりましたから……

と言った。これは喫茶用のテーブルのほうへ移動してほしいということで、言葉

she did not verbally say so. Japanese usually do not say *nonde-kudasai* (please drink it) or *nomi-ni kite-kudasai* (please come to drink it) after *Ocha-ga hairimashita* (The tea is ready).

The next day, when Mr. Lerner went to see Mr. Okada at his office. Miss Hayashi, his secretary, said to them

Ocha-ga hairimashita-kedo . . .
(lit., The tea is ready, but . . .)

implying that she wanted them to come to where the tea was served.

Since Mr. Lerner was paying special attention to how Japanese end their sentences, he noticed that the two women had used different sentence endings, *kara* (because) and *kedo* (but), in similar situations. To him these two seem so apart from each other in meaning that he can't understand how they can be used for the same purpose.

*   *   *

Kara and *kedo* are used with quite different meanings in factual statements, as in the following examples:

Ame-ga furimashita-kara ikimasen-deshita.
(Because it rained we didn't go.)
Ame-ga furimashita-kedo ikimashita.
(It rained but we went.)

But in making requests or asking about someone else's wishes, *kara* and *kedo* seem to be used in a similar way. Both *Ocha-ga hairimashita-kara* and *Ocha-ga hairimashita-kedo* can precede *doozo kite-kudasai* (please come), although this is usually left out. The two endings, however, reflect different attitudes on the part of the speaker. When he says . . . *kara*, he is asking someone to do him a favor as a matter of course. On the other hand, if he

ではそう言わないが、お茶を飲んでくれという意味である。日本語では「お茶が
はいりましたから」のあとに、「飲んでください」とか「飲みに来てください」
などは、言わないですませるのが普通である。

　こうした事情のわかってきた Mr. Lerner であるが、次の日 Mr. Okada の会社
をたずねると、秘書の Miss Hayashi が、やはりお茶の用意のしてあるところへ
移動してほしいということを、

　　　お茶がはいりましたけど……

という文で伝えたのである。

　日本語の文末がどうなるか、特別の注意を払ってきただけに、同じ状況で2人
の女性が異なる文末「から」と「けど」を使ったことに、Mr. Lerner はすぐ気が
ついた。この2つは意味からいって全く正反対と思われるのに、どうして同じ目
的に使われるのか、理解に苦しむ事実だと彼は思った……。

＊　　　　　＊　　　　　＊

「から」と「けど」は、事実の叙述においては全く別の意味をもつ。

　　　雨が降りましたから、行きませんでした
　　　雨が降りましたけど、行きました

は全く異なる。

　しかし、人に何か依頼したり人の希望をたずねたりする時は、「から」と「け
ど」は同じように用いられる観がある。「お茶がはいりましたから」も「お茶が
はいりましたけど」も、「どうぞ来てください」の前につけることができる。
（もっとも「どうぞ来てください」は省かれるのが普通であるが。）しかし、こ
の2つの文末に反映している話し手の態度は、全く違っている。「〜から」と言
う時は、当然のこととして人に何か依頼するのであるが、「〜けど」の場合は、
依頼をためらう気持ちが表されている。この「〜けど」を敷衍して言えば、「こ

says . . . *kedo*, it shows that he is hesitant about making the request; in this case *kedo* can be paraphrased as "I know I shouldn't trouble you, but." Thus, generally speaking, sentences ending in . . . *kedo* sound more polite than those ending in . . . *kara*.

You can urge someone to start something either by saying

Moo jikan-desu-kara . . .

(Because it's already time, . . .)

or

Moo jikan-desu-kedo . . .

(It's already time, but . . .)

The latter sounds more polite and is usually preferred.

(*Keredomo* and *keredo* are sometimes used in place of *kedo* without changing the meaning; *kedo* is more conversational and familiar.)

(July 30, 1978)

Ato-de kekkoo-desu-kara
あとで けっこうですから
Because it's all right to do it later

A few days ago Miss Yoshida asked Mr. Lerner to help her with her work. She said that it wouldn't take long, adding

Ato-de kekkoo-desu-kara.

(lit., Because it's all right to do it later.)

148

んなお願いをすべきではないのですけど」となる。したがって、一般に、「〜け
ど」のほうが「〜から」よりも丁寧にひびく。

　何か始めるように人をうながす時、

　　　もう時間ですから……

とも、

　　　もう時間ですけど……

とも言う。後者のほうが丁寧な言いかたとして歓迎される。

　（なお、「けれども」「けれど」も同じ意味で使われるが、「けど」のほうが会話
的でくだけた感じがする。）

（1978.7.30）

あとでけっこうですから

Because it's all right to do it later

　2、3日前、Miss Yoshida が Mr. Lerner に仕事を手伝ってくれと頼んだが、
その時、あまり時間はかからないと言ったあとで、

　　　あとでけっこうですから

とつけ加えた。

Mr. Lerner understood that she had added this out of consideration in not wanting to inconvenience him, but he didn't quite understand why she had ended the sentence with *kara*.

This reminded him of Sensee telling him that Japanese often use *kara* when it does not mean "because." They will say something like

Ocha-ga hairimashita-kara doozo.

(Tea is ready. Please come and have some.)

If you translate this as "Because tea is ready, please come," it will sound strange. He also had heard Mr. Takada saying to Miss Yoshida

Ashita kaesu-kara sen-en kashite.

(lit., Because I'm going to return it tomorrow, lend me ¥1,000.)

*　　　　　*　　　　　*

Kara is used to give a reason just as "because" or "since" does, but the reason indicated by the phrase with *kara* does not necessarily concern a fact. In other words, *kara* in *Kane-ga nai-kara kaenai* (Because I don't have the money, I can't buy it) concerns a factual reason. The reason for not being able to buy something is the fact that the speaker doesn't have enough money. But *kara* is also used to indicate the reason why the speaker wants to do something.

Ato-de kekkoo-desu-kara, tetsudatte-kudasai.

can be paraphrased as "I know that you are busy and I feel I shouldn't trouble you, so I'm saying that you don't have to do it right now but that you can do it later. BECAUSE I'm being so considerate I think I can be allowed to ask you to help me." In short, *Ato-de kekkoo-desu-kara* is used to justify the speaker's making the request rather than to explain why the

Mr. Lerner は、この言葉が、面倒をかけまいという彼女の配慮から出たものであることはわかったが、なぜ文の終わりに「から」をつけたのか理解できなかった。

その後、Mr. Lerner は、日本人の使う「から」は "because" の意味ではないと、先生が言っていたことを思い出した。

　　　お茶がはいりましたから、どうぞ

というような場合、"Because tea is ready, please come." と直訳したら、変に聞こえる。また、いつか Mr. Takada が Miss Yoshida に、

　　　あした返すから、千円貸して

と言っていたのも、同じことだ……。

＊　　　　　＊　　　　　＊

「から」には "because" や "since" と同じように理由を示す働きがある。しかし「から」のついた句は必ずしも事実に関して使われるのではない。たとえば、「金がないから買えない」は、事実の理由を示している。買うことができないことの理由は、金を十分持っていないことである。しかし「から」はまた、話し手がなぜそれを希望するかという理由を示すのにも用いられる。

　　　あとでけっこうですから、手伝ってください

を敷衍すれば、「お忙しいことはわかっているし、ご面倒をおかけすべきでないと思います。それで、今でなくあとでやってくだされればいいと言っているのです。このように気を使っているのですから、お願いしても許されると思います」となる。要するに、「あとでけっこうですから」は、手助けを望む理由を説明するのではなく、依頼そのものを正当化するために、用いられているのである。同様に、Mr. Takada が言った、「あした返すから千円貸して」の「あした返すから」

speaker wants someone to help him. In the same way, in Mr. Takada's sentence *Ashita kaesu-kara sen-en kashite,* *Ashita kaesu-kara* is said to justify his request.

Using *kara* is avoided when one should not openly justify oneself. For instance, when asked why you are late, it's more polite to say

Densha-ga okuremashita-node.

(Because the train was late.)

Node is used to objectively state a reason and is also used on more formal occasions. If you said

Densha-ga okuremashita-kara.

it would imply that you are asking to be spared criticism.

(February 26, 1978)

Gomennasai

ごめんなさい

I'm sorry

At the office where Mr. Lerner works, a reception was held yesterday afternoon in honor of an important visitor. Mr. Lerner was asked to give a

も、自分の依頼を正当化するものである。

　正面から正当化してはならない時には、「から」の使用は避ける。たとえば遅刻した理由をたずねられた時は、

　　　電車がおくれましたので

と言うほうが礼儀正しい。「ので」は理由を客観的に述べるのに用いられるとされ、したがって改まった場面でも用いられる。

　　　電車がおくれましたから

と言うと、批判しないでもらいたいという気持ちが含まれる。

> ▶英語の "because" などは事実関係を示すのに用いられるが、「から」は話者の心情にかかわるので「主観的」という説明も当たっている。ただし、「から」の自己正当化は必ずしも自己主張ではなく依頼などでの思いやりを示すのにも用いられることに留意。

(1978.2.26)

ごめんなさい

I'm sorry

　Mr. Lerner の勤めている会社では、昨日の午後、大事なお客を歓迎するためのパーティーが開かれた。Mr. Lerner も日本語で簡単なスピーチをすることになっ

short speech in Japanese. Since everybody looked very formal, he became rather nervous and made a mistake in pronouncing the guest's name, so he hurriedly apologized, saying

Gomennasai.
(I'm sorry.)

Many of the people there laughed. This helped the people relax, although Mr. Lerner lost some confidence in his Japanese.

Later Mr. Takada said that they had laughed because *Gomennasai* sounds feminine; Miss Yoshida said that it was because the expression sounds childish.

*　　　*　　　*

Mr. Lerner should have said

Shitsuree-shimashita.
(lit., I was rude.)

instead of *Gomennasai*. *Gomennasai* is one of those expressions that are used mostly at home between family members, while *Shitsuree-shimashita* is used in social situations. Little children usually apologize to their parents or teachers by saying *Gomennasai*, but *Shitsuree-shimashita* is not usually used between family members. (*Sumimasen* is also used in apology. It is less formal than *Shitsuree-shimashita* and is used both inside and outside of one's home, by adults or older boys and girls; if a little child said *Sumimasen* to his parents it would sound rather strange.)

Outside of the home, *Gomennasai* is used mainly in family-like situations. Most often it is used by children; among adults, it is often used in informal conversation. For instance, a child will say it to a stranger whose foot he has stepped on by mistake in the train. An elderly person may say

た。全員がかしこまっているので彼も固くなり、お客の名前を言い違えてしまった。そこであわてて、

　　ゴメンナサイ

と言ってしまった。笑い声が起こって、雰囲気はなごやかになったが、Mr. Lerner は日本語に対する自信を失ってしまった。

　あとで Mr. Takada が、みんなが笑ったのは「ごめんなさい」は女性的だからだと言った。Miss Yoshida は、いや、子供っぽいからだと反論した……。

＊　　　　　　＊　　　　　　＊

　Mr. Lerner が「ごめんなさい」の代わりに、

　　失礼しました

と言っていたら、問題はなかったであろう。「失礼しました」が社会的な場面で使われるのに対して、「ごめんなさい」は主として家庭の中で使われる表現である。小さい子供が親や教師にあやまる時は普通「ごめんなさい」と言うが、「失礼しました」は通常家族の間では使わない。（「すみません」も詫びる時の表現である。「失礼しました」ほど改まっておらず、家庭の中でも外でも使われるが、主に成人や青少年に用いられる。小さい子供が親に「すみません」と言うのは異様である。）

　家庭外でも、家庭的な場面であれば、「ごめんなさい」が使われる。大抵は子供であるが、成人でも気楽な話し合いでは使うことがある。たとえば子供が電車の中で、知らない人の足をうっかりふんだ場合など、「ごめんなさい」を使うし、年配の人が若い人に対する時は、会社の中であっても、改まった場合でなければ使う。

　「失礼しました」のような改まった、あるいは社会でのみ用いられる表現と、「ごめんなさい」のような親しい間での表現との区別は、次第にゆるやかになっ

it to a younger person even when working at the office unless he has to be formal.

The distinction between formal or social expressions such as *Shitsuree-shimashita* and familiar expressions such as *Gomennasai* seems to be becoming looser. Some people have started using familiar expressions, either intentionally or unintentionally, in formal or social situations. But still it is important to choose appropriate expressions according to the situation if you want to be a really good speaker of Japanese.

(December 25, 1977)

Warui-desu-ne
わるいですね
I'm sorry

When Mr. Lerner was taking a walk in the vicinity of the office yesterday noon, he saw two young men playing catch in the street, perhaps making the most of their lunch time. He stood and watched them for a while. When one of the players threw the ball too high and the other had to run for it, the pitcher said

Aa, warui, warui.
(Sorry! —lit., Oh, bad, bad.)

Mr. Lerner had sometimes heard Miss Yoshida say *Warui-n-desu-kedo . . .*

156

て行くようである。改まった場面でも、意図するにせよしないにせよ、親しい表現を用いる人も出てきた。しかし、真に良き日本語の使い手となるためには、やはり場面に応じて適切な表現を選ぶことが重要である。

(1977.12.25)

わるいですね

I'm sorry

　昨日の昼ごろに Mr. Lerner が会社の近くを散歩していると、2人の若い男が昼休みを利用して通りでキャッチボールをしていた。一方がボールを高く投げすぎてしまい、相手が走ってとりに行った。すると投げたほうが、

　　ああ、わるい、わるい

と言った。

　Miss Yoshida がときどき「わるいんですけど」と言うのは聞いたが、このように「わるい」と言うのは聞いたことがなかった。いったい日本語には詫びの表現がいくつあるのだろうと Mr. Lerner は考えた。「すみません」「ごめんなさい」

(I'm sorry but . . .) but had never heard *warui* used in this way. He wondered just how many expressions Japanese use to apologize; he had learned *sumimasen*, *gomennasai*, *shitsuree-shimashita*, and *mooshiwake arimasen*, but there seemed to be still more.

*   *   *

Warui literally means "bad." It is used as an apology meaning "I shouldn't do this" or "I shouldn't have done that." *Warui-desu-ne* is used as an apology like *sumimasen*, but it is more familiar than *sumimasen*. Saying just *Warui*, like the two young men Mr. Lerner saw playing catch, is limited to very familiar conversations.

Among various expressions used for apology, *sumimasen* is used most widely; when you have to be very polite or formal you should say *Shitsuree-shimashita* or *Mooshiwake arimasen*. When the speaker feels that his offense was serious, he says *Mooshiwake arimasen*. When compared with these expressions *Warui-desu-ne* sounds more familiar and casual. A father will apologize to his child saying

> *Warui-ne* or *Warukatta-ne.*

A mother will say

> *Warui-wane* or *Warukatta-wane.*

although some mothers use *gomennasai* more often. But a child will not say *Warui-ne* to senior members of his family. He is supposed to say *Gomennasai* instead.

(February 24, 1980)

「失礼しました」「申し訳ありません」などなど。そのほかにもまだあるらしいの
だ……。

＊　　　　　　　＊　　　　　　　＊

「わるい」は文字通りには "bad" であるが、詫びの言葉としては「こんなこと
をすべきではない」「あんなことをすべきではなかった」の意味になる。「わるい
ですね」は「すみません」と同じように詫びる時使われるが、「すみません」よ
りくだけた感じがする。Mr. Lerner が通った時キャッチボールをしていた2人の
青年が使ったように、ただ「わるい」と言いきるのはごく親しい間での表現であ
る。

詫びに用いられる言葉の中で、もっとも広く用いられるのは「すみません」で
ある。改まった時や丁寧に話すべき時は、「失礼しました」「申し訳ありません」
を使う。自分のおかした非礼が重大であると感じた場合には「申し訳ありませ
ん」を用いる。こうした表現にくらべると「わるいですね」はくだけた、気楽な
感じを与える。父親が子供に詫びる時は、

　　　わるいね
　　　わるかったね

などを用いる。母親なら、

　　　わるいわね
　　　わるかったわね

と言う。もっとも母親の場合には「ごめんなさい」を多く使う者もいる。しかし
子供は年上の家族に対して「わるいね」とは言わない。「ごめんなさい」と言う
ようにしつけられる。

（1980.2.24）

Zannen-desu-ne
ざんねんですね
That's too bad

Mr. Lerner often finds it difficult to give an appropriate comment on someone's statement. For instance, when he heard that Mr. Okada's daughter had found a job, he wondered if he should say *Omedetoo-gozaimasu* (Congratulations!) or *Yokatta-desu-ne* (That's good, isn't it?). While he was wondering, Mr. Okada apparently thought that he had not understood, and repeated his statement, to Mr. Lerner's irritation. Later Mr. Takada said that one can say either of the two, or even both as

Omedetoo-gozaimasu. Yokatta-desu-ne.
(The first sounds more formal than the second.)

Then a few days later, he had a hard time trying to find a good expression when Mr. Okada told him that his son had had a traffic accident. He finally said

Zannen-desu-ne.

Mr. Okada politely thanked him for his sympathy, but he felt that his comment was awkward somehow.

*   *   *

Zannen-desu-ne is used when the speaker has been disappointed by something, and thinks that the person involved must be disappointed too.

残念ですね

That's too bad

　人の話に適切な応答をするのはむずかしいものだと、Mr. Lerner は思う。たとえば Mr. Okada の娘さんが就職したと聞いた時、「おめでとうございます」と言うべきか、「よかったですね」と言うべきか、迷っていると、Mr. Okada は、話がわからなかったのだと思ったらしく、もう一度言い直す始末で、実にいらいらした。あとで Mr. Takada にきいてみると、そのどちらでもいいし、

　　おめでとうございます。よかったですね

と重ねてもよいとのことだった。
　その数日後、Mr. Okada が、息子が交通事故にあったと言った時も、いい言葉がなかなか見つからず苦しんだあげく、

　　残念デスネ

と言ってしまった。Mr. Okada はこの同情の言葉に対して丁重に礼を述べたが、やはりこれもまずかったのだろうと Mr. Lerner は思った……。

＊　　　　　＊　　　　　＊

　「残念ですね」は、話し手が何かに失望し、当事者も失望したろうと思った時に用いる。したがって、だれかが試験に失敗した時や希望が実現しなかった時は、この言葉が適切である。しかし、交通事故のような場合は、失望すべき事柄ではなく、不幸が起こったのであるから、「残念ですね」とは言わない。事故が

Therefore, when someone has failed in his exams or realizing his wishes, it is proper to say this. But this expression is not used in the case of a traffic accident or the like, because that is not a matter of disappointment but of misfortune. If the accident is not very serious and only causes some trouble, one says

Taihen-desu-ne.

(It must be tough.)

If the accident has caused injury or sickness, one says

Sore-wa ikemasen-ne. Odaiji-ni.

(That's too bad. Take good care of yourself.)

This expression can be used when someone has caught a cold or been taken ill.

But when the accident has caused death, or in other cases of bereavement, one usually expresses his surprise and sorrow by other means. As verbal expressions, there are such phrases as

Goshuushoosama-desu.

(Deepest condolences.)

or

Kono tabi-wa tonda koto-de . . .

(This time it is really terrible . . .)

But usually one just says *Soo-desu-ka . . .* (Is that so?) or *Hontoo-desu-ka* (Is that true?) in an almost whispering voice. In such cases, nonverbal expressions such as dropping one's shoulders or looking down are more important. Fluent comments, especially accompanied by inappropriate nonverbal expressions, are rather damaging.

(December 5, 1978)

あまりひどいものでなく、大した問題にもならなければ、

　　　　大変ですね

と言う。
　その事故が障害や病気を起こした場合は、

　　　　それはいけませんね。お大事に

と言う。この表現はかぜをひいた人や病気になった人にも言う。
　しかし、事故が死につながった場合や、家族を失った場合などは、その驚きと悲しみは他の方法で表す。悲しみの言葉としては、

　　　　ご愁傷さまです
　　　　この度はとんだことで……

などの決まり文句があるが、ただ「そうですか」「ほんとうですか」など、ほとんど聞きとれぬような声で言うだけの場合も多い。こうした場合、肩を落とすとかうつむくというような、身体による表現が大切である。雄弁な話しぶり、それも身体の表現が不適切である場合など、かえって逆効果となる。

（1978.11.5）

Kaetta hoo-ga ii

帰った ほうが いい

You had better go home

Mr. Lerner noticed that Miss Yoshida did not look well when she was typing yesterday afternoon. When he asked her if she was all right, she said that she had caught a cold, so he said

Moo kaeru hoo-ga ii-desu-yo.

meaning "You had better go home now." Then Mr. Takada came and joined him, saying

Moo kaetta hoo-ga ii-yo.

Mr. Lerner wondered if he should have said *kaetta* instead of *kaeru*.

*   *   *

Both *Kaeru hoo-ga ii* and *Kaetta hoo-ga ii* are grammatically correct, but the speaker's attitude is different. When one says *Kaeru hoo-ga ii*, he states his judgment; he thinks that going home is better than not going home. On the other hand, when one says *Kaetta hoo-ga ii*, he is advising the listener to go home.

In this way, verbs in the past form are used to give advice, as in

Sugu dekaketa hoo-ga ii-deshoo.

(You had better leave right away.)

帰ったほうがいい

You had better go home

　きのうの午後、Miss Yoshida がタイプをしているところを見ると、どうも調子が悪そうなので、Mr. Lerner は大丈夫かとたずねた。彼女がかぜをひいたと答えたので、

　　　モウ帰ルホウガイイデスヨ

と言った。そこへ Mr. Takada も来て、

　　　もう帰ったほうがいいよ

と言った。

　「帰る」でなく「帰った」と言うべきだったのだろうかと、Mr. Lerner は思った……。

＊　　　　　＊　　　　　＊

　「帰るほうがいい」も「帰ったほうがいい」も文法的には正しいが、話し手の態度が異なる。「帰るほうがいい」というのは判断の表明である。家へ帰ることは、帰らないことよりよいという判断を示している。それに対して「帰ったほうがいい」は、帰ることを相手にすすめる表現である。

　このように、過去形の動詞は助言を与えるのに用いられ、

　　　すぐ出かけたほうがいいでしょう

165

Kusuri-o nonda hoo-ga ii-desu-yo.
(You had better take some medicine.)

It is not easy to give advice politely. When one uses this ... *ta (da) hoo-ga ii* expression in polite situations, one has to change the verb into the *o ... -ni naru* form as in

Sugu odekake-ni natta hoo-ga ii-deshoo.
(It might be better if you left right away.)

And sometimes the last part of the sentence is also changed as in

Kusuri-o onomi-ni natta hoo-ga yoroshii-ka-to omoimasu.
(It might be better if you took some medicine.)

Or, one often avoids using ... *ta (da) hoo-ga ii* and uses some other expression instead such as

Sugu odekake-ni nattara ikaga-deshoo.
(Wouldn't it be better if you left right away?)
Kusuri-o onomi-ni natte-wa ikaga-deshoo.
(Wouldn't it be better if you took some medicine?)

(April 10, 1983)

　　　薬を飲んだほうがいいですよ

のように言う。

　人に助言する時、失礼にならないようにするのは容易ではない。「〜た（だ）ほうがいい」を丁寧な話の中で用いるには、動詞を「お〜になる」に直して、

　　　すぐお出かけになったほうがいいでしょう

としなければならない。また文の最後の部分も変えて、

　　　薬をお飲みになったほうがよろしいかと思います

のようにする。

　また、「〜た（だ）ほうがいい」を使うのを避けて、ほかの表現を用いることも多い。

　　　すぐお出かけになったらいかがでしょう
　　　薬をお飲みになってはいかがでしょう

などである。

（1983.4.10）

Taihen kekkoo-da-to omoimasu
たいへん けっこうだと おもいます
I think it's very good

Yesterday afternoon the director of the company, Mr. Mori, asked Mr. Lerner and Mr. Takada to come to his office, and explained his plan for developing a new system to improve the company's business. When he finished his explanation and asked the two men to comment on it, Mr. Takada said

Taihen kekkoo-da-to omoimasu.
(I think it's very good.)

So Mr. Lerner thought that there would be no further discussion between Mr. Mori and Mr. Takada, and that it was his turn to state his opinion. When he was about to do so, Mr. Mori asked Mr. Takada again if there was any respect in which it could be improved. Then Mr. Takada said

Soo-desu-nee . . .
(Well . . .)

and paused. Mr. Mori prompted him to continue. Mr. Takada said

Machigatte-iru-kamo shiremasen-ga . . .
(I may be wrong but . . .)

Mr. Mori told him that he should stop worrying and go ahead.
Finally Mr. Takada pointed out one place that he thought might be

たいへん結構だと思います

I think it's very good

　昨日の午後、社長の Mr. Mori に呼ばれて、Mr. Lerner と Mr. Takada が社長室へ行くと、社長は社の営業成績をあげる新体制開発の計画の説明を始めた。説明が終わって2人の意見をたずねられたが、Mr. Takada は、

　　たいへん結構だと思います

と言った。Mr. Lerner は、もう Mr. Takada は意見を述べ終わって、今度は自分の番だと思ったので、何か言おうとしたが、Mr. Mori は再び Mr. Takada に向かって、どこか改めるところはないかとたずねた。すると Mr. Takada は、

　　そうですねえ……

と言ってからしばらく黙っていたが、Mr. Mori が先をうながすと、

　　間違っているかもしれませんが……

と言った。Mr. Mori はそんな心配はしないで思い切って言えと言った。

　ようやく Mr. Takada は、改善すべきだと思う点を指摘した。Mr. Lerner は、今度こそ Mr. Takada の話は終わって自分の番だと思った。ところがどっこい、Mr. Mori はまた Mr. Takada に向かって、ほかに直すところはないかときくのだ……！

＊　　　　　＊　　　　　＊

changed. Mr. Lerner thought that now Mr. Takada was finished and it was his turn, but it wasn't. Mr. Mori again wondered if there were any other points that Mr. Takada thought should be revised!

*   *   *

It is not easy to criticize someone else without hurting his feelings in any society, but it takes more time and consideration in polite conversation in Japanese. When someone has made a proposal and invites criticism, one usually first expresses one's appreciation; Mr. Takada first said that he thought the plan to be very good. And when one is urged to state his opinion, he does not immediately start stating it but shows his hesitation, as Mr. Takada did in saying *Soo-desu-nee*. Mr. Mori again prompted him but he indicated his apprehension that he might be wrong in order to ascertain that Mr. Mori was fully ready for his criticism.

Our students often ask what expressions should be used to state their criticism politely in Japanese, but mere repetition of verbal expressions will not work. It is much more important to try to find the right moment when one can express himself without damaging his good relations with the listener.

(December 17, 1978)

　どの社会でも、感情を傷つけることなくその人の批判をすることは容易なことではないが、日本語の丁寧な会話では、特に時間をかけ、気を配ることが必要である。だれかが提案をして批判を求めた時は、まずその案を高く評価する。Mr. Takada がたいへんよい案だと思うと言ったのは、これである。提案者に意見を求められても、すぐには意見を述べず躊躇を示す。Mr. Takada が「そうですねえ……」と言ったのはこれである。Mr. Mori が再度うながした時、間違っているかもしれないという危惧を示したのは、Mr. Mori に批判を受け入れる態勢を十分に作らせるためである。

　日本語で丁寧に批判を述べるには、どんな言葉を使えばよいか、と外国人の学習者がよくたずねる。しかし単に丁寧な言葉を積み重ねるだけでは丁寧にならない。重要なのは、相手との関係をそこなうことなく意見の言える適切な瞬間を見出そうと努力することである。

（1978.12.17）

Konna jikan-ni sumimasen
こんな 時間に すみません
I'm sorry to trouble you at such an hour

Mr. Okada called Mr. Lerner at his office yesterday afternoon around five o'clock. He started by saying

Konna jikan-ni sumimasen-ga . . .
(lit., I'm sorry at such an hour, but . . .)

Mr. Lerner said that he didn't mind at all, but it took him some time to realize that Mr. Okada was sorry for calling him when he must be getting ready to leave the office. He remembered that many Japanese start talking on the phone with an apology of some kind or other. He wished he had listened to them more carefully so that he could use such apologies himself.

*　　　　*　　　　*

The basic form of apology is *. . . te sumimasen* as in *osoku natte sumimasen* (I'm sorry I'm late). The whole sentence should be, in Mr. Okada's utterance above, *Konna jikan-ni denwa-shite sumimasen* (I'm sorry to call you at such an hour); *denwa-shite* is understood and left out.

It is polite to apologize for disturbing someone by calling him at an inconvenient time, although it is rather difficult to know what time would be convenient for the listener. Usually at an early hour one says

こんな時間にすみません

I'm sorry to trouble you at such an hour

　Mr. Lerner が昨日会社で仕事をしていると、5時ごろ Mr. Okada から電話がかかってきた。Mr. Okada はまず、

　　こんな時間にすみませんが……

と言った。

　Mr. Lerner は「かまいませんよ」と答えたが、退社の準備をするころに電話したことを詫びているのだということが、とっさにはわからなかった。そういえば日本人はよく電話口でこうした詫びを言う。ふだんからもっと気をつけて聞いていて、自分でもそのような詫びごとが言えるようにしておけばよかったと、Mr. Lerner は思った……。

＊　　　　　　＊　　　　　　＊

　詫びの表現の基本的な形は「～てすみません」で、「おそくなってすみません」のように使う。Mr. Okada の述べた詫びは、全部言えば、「こんな時間に電話してすみません」ということで、「電話して」は当然言わなくてもわかるものとして省かれている。

　都合のわるい時間に電話することによって迷惑をかける時には、詫びるのが礼儀であるが、相手にとってどの時間が好都合かを知るのはむずかしいことも事実である。通常、朝早い場合には、

Konna-ni asa hayaku sumimasen.

(Sorry to call you at such an early hour as this in the morning.)

And late at night one says

Konna-ni yoru osoku sumimasen.

(Sorry to call you at such a late hour as this at night.)

In both of these sentences *Konna-ni* can be left out. At mealtime one says

Oshokuji-no jikan-ni . . .

(. . . at mealtime.)

And in all these instances, one can say

Konna jikan-ni . . .

(. . . at such an hour.)

These expressions are used not only when telephoning but also when visiting someone. There are several other common expressions for apologizing for disturbing someone at an inconvenient time. Some expressions have *tokoro-o* (while) as in

oisogashii tokoro-o . . .

(when you're busy . . .)

or

oyasumi-no tokoro-o . . .

(when you're resting . . .) (See pp. 192-194.)

There are some other expressions with *chuu* (in the midst of) as in

oshigoto-chuu . . . (when you're at work . . .)
oshokuji-chuu . . . (when you're eating . . .)

or

> こんなに朝早くすみません

と言い、夜には、

> こんなに夜おそくすみません

と言う。どちらの場合にも「こんなに」を省いてもよい。
　食事どきには、

> お食事の時間に……

と言う。
　以上のいずれの場合にも、

> こんな時間に……

を使うことができる。
　こうした表現は、電話をする場合だけでなく、人を訪問する時にも用いられる。都合のわるい時間に人を訪問する時の詫びの言葉には、その他いくつかある。「ところ」を使った、

> お忙しいところを……
> お休みのところを……　　　　（193 ページ参照）

や、「中」を使った、

> お仕事中……
> お食事中……
> ご勉強中……

などがある。

gobenkyoo-chuu . . . (when you're studying . . .)

When you have to interrupt someone engaged in conversation with someone else, you can say

Ohanashi-chuu sumimasen-ga . . .

(I'm sorry to interrupt you when you're talking with someone . . .)

(May 18, 1980)

Taihen-desu-ne
たいへんですね
That's tough

One Friday evening, Mr. Lerner had finished his work and was about to leave the office, but Mr. Takada was still working. He wanted to express his sympathy for Mr. Takada's having to work on Friday evening and was wondering what the appropriate expression would be when Miss Yoshida went by and said,

Taihen-desu-ne.

(That's tough. —lit., It's terrible, isn't it?)

Mr. Takada smiled and said there wasn't much left to do and asked her not to worry.

A few days later, on a cold morning Mr. Lerner saw Mr. Okada, his neighbor, busy washing his car. He tried this expression *Taihen-desu-ne.* It

人と話をしている時に中断を求める時は、

　　　お話し中すみませんが……

と言う。

（1980.5.18）

大変ですね

That's tough

　金曜日の夕方、Mr. Lerner が仕事を終えて会社を出ようとしてふと見ると、Mr. Takada はまだ仕事中であった。金曜の夕方なのに帰れないことに対する同情を表したいと思ったが、何と言えばいいのかと迷っていると、Miss Yoshida が通りかかって、

　　　大変ですね

と言った。Mr. Takada はにっこりして、もうすぐ終わるからご心配なく、と答えた。

　２、３日後の寒い朝、Mr. Lerner はお隣のご主人がせっせと車を洗っているのを見たので、「大変ですね」を使ってみた。効果は絶大であった。彼は満面に笑みを浮かべて、

produced a great effect. Mr. Okada smiled in a very friendly manner and said,

> *Raanaa-san-koso, samui-noni taihen-desu-ne.*
> (It's you, Mr. Lerner, that's having a terrible time when it's so cold.)

*   *   *

The word *taihen* means "unusual" or "terrible"; it can mean "an unusually hard job" or "a terrible experience." You can use this word to refer to your own condition or experience, for example,

> *Mainichi taihen-desu.*
> (I'm terribly busy every day.)

or

> *Kinoo-wa taihen-deshita.*
> (I had a terrible experience yesterday.)

The expression *Taihen-desu-ne* is often used in everyday conversation to show sympathy. You may have noticed that Japanese use this expression towards people working hard—businessmen working overtime, students studying hard to get into a good college, waitresses during the lunch-time rush, and so on.

The Japanese like to show respect for diligence even if a person may be working hard for his own personal benefit. They wish to build up good relations with others by expressing their appreciation of diligence and their sympathy for having to work hard.

(February 13, 1977)

　　　ラーナーさんこそ、寒いのに大変ですね

と言った……。

＊　　　　　＊　　　　　＊

　「大変」という語は「普通ではない」とか「ひどい」という意味を持ち、「極めて困難な仕事」「ひどい経験」などを指す。自分自身の状態や経験についても、この語を用いて、

　　　毎日大変です

とか、

　　　きのうは大変でした

などと言う。
　「大変ですね」は、日常生活で他人に対する同情を表すのによく用いられる。一生懸命働いている人——残業中のサラリーマン、大学受験のために勉強中の学生、昼食時でいそがしいウエートレスなど——に対するねぎらいの言葉として「大変ですね」がよく使われる。
　たとえ自分自身のために働くのであっても、営々と働く人に対しては、日本人は尊敬を示すのが好きである。相手の勤勉さをほめ、苦労に同情することによって、良き人間関係を築きたいと願うからである。

（1977.2.13）

Taishita koto-wa arimasen
たいした ことは ありません
It's nothing

When everyone was getting ready to leave the office yesterday evening, Mr. Takada was still working busily. He had something he had to finish that day. Mr. Lerner expressed his sympathy for him by saying *Taihen-desu-ne* (It's rough, isn't it?). Then Mr. Takada replied

Iie, taishita koto-wa arimasen.

(No, it's nothing.)

Mr. Lerner remembered that he had always been saying *Iie* or *Iie, daijoobu-desu* (No, it's all right) in this kind of situation, and thought he should use this expression next time.

*   *   *

Taishita koto-wa arimasen literally means "It's not anything of great extent"; it is used to deny that something is of high degree. For instance, when someone asks you if the play you saw was good, you might say *Taishita koto-wa arimasen-deshita* to mean "It wasn't very good." In daily conversation, one of its frequent usages is to respond to someone's expression of sympathy as in the instance above. One uses this expression not only for work, but also when referring to sickness or fatigue, as in

A: *Taihen-deshita-ne. Otsukare-deshoo.*
(That was tough. You must be tired.)

大したことはありません

It's nothing

　昨日の夕方、みなそろって社を出ようとした時、Mr. Takada はまだせっせと仕事をしていた。どうしてもその日にすませなければならないことがあったのだろう。Mr. Lerner は「タイヘンデスネ」と同情の意を表したが、Mr. Takada は、

　　　いいえ、大したことはありません

と答えた。このような場合、これまでいつも「イイエ」とか「イイエ、ダイジョウブデス」と言ってきたが、今度からはこの返事にしようと Mr. Lerner は思った……。

＊　　　　　　＊　　　　　　＊

　「大したことはありません」は文字通りには、「程度の進んだものではない」の意味で、程度の高さを否定するのに用いられる。たとえば、芝居を見たそうだがどうだったかときかれた場合、「大したことはありませんでした」と言えば、「あまりよくなかった」の意味になる。日常生活でよく使われるのは、上の場合のように、だれかの同情に答える時である。これは仕事の場合だけでなく、病気や疲労にも用いられる。

　　Ａ：大変でしたね。お疲れでしょう
　　Ｂ：いいえ、大したことはありません。ご心配なく

この表現はまた、人にほめられた時にも用いられる。

B: *Iie, taishita koto-wa arimasen. Goshinpai naku.*
 (No, it's nothing. Please don't worry.)

This expression is also used for responding to someone's compliment like

Nihongo-ga ojoozu-desu-ne.
(You speak Japanese very well.)

You can deny it by saying something like

Iie, sonna koto-wa arimasen.
(No, it's no such thing.)

or

Iie, tondemo arimasen.
(No, not at all.)

But these are complete denial. When you have to admit the truth of the compliment to some extent, you can say

Iie, taishita koto-wa arimasen.
(No, I'm not very good.)

or

Sorehodo-demo arimasen.
(lit., It's not to the extent you say.)

(May 11, 1980)

　　　日本語がお上手ですね

と言われた時、

　　　いいえ、そんなことはありません

とか、

　　　いいえ、とんでもありません

のように否定することもできる。しかし、こうした答えは完全な否定になってしまう。ほめ言葉がある程度事実であることを認めざるを得ない時は、

　　　いいえ、大したことはありません

とか、

　　　それほどでもありません

と答えてもよい。

（1980.5.11）

Okagesama-de
おかげさまで
Thanks to you

The other day Mr. Lerner helped Mr. Takada with his work after finishing his own. Mr. Takada thanked him by saying,

Okagesama-de hayaku sumimashita.
(I finished quickly thanks to your help.)

A few days later, when Mr. Lerner asked Mr. Okada, his neighbor, if his son had passed the college entrance exam, he answered,

Hai, okagesama-de.
(Yes, thank you. —lit., Yes, thanks to you.)

Mr. Lerner felt it strange to be thanked when he had not done anything to help Mr. Okada's son.

*   *   *

Okagesama-de is used to express gratitude either to a particular person or to all that has been helpful.

A grateful patient will say to his doctor

Okagesama-de yoku narimashita.
(Thanks to you, I've recovered.)

And also when an acquaintance asks how he feels, he will say,

おかげさまで

Thanks to you

　先日、Mr. Lerner は自分の仕事が終わったあと、Mr. Takada の仕事を手伝った。Mr. Takada は感謝して、

　　おかげさまで早くすみました

と言った。その数日後、隣家の主人に会ったので、息子さんは大学入試に受かったかとたずねると、

　　はい、おかげさまで

と答えた。

　この場合は何も手伝ったわけでないのに、どうしてお礼を言われるのかと、Mr. Lerner は不思議に思った……。

＊　　　　＊　　　　＊

「おかげさまで」は、特定の人に対する感謝にも、すべての力に対する感謝にも用いられる。

　患者は医者に感謝して、

　　おかげさまで、よくなりました

と言うし、知人に健康状態をたずねられた時も、

Okagesama-de yoku narimashita.

He doesn't mean that the acquaintance has helped him recover from the illness; he means that he feels grateful for all the factors that have made his recovery possible, including the acquaintance.

This expression *Okagesama-de* is sometimes used simply as a formality in such exchanges as

A: *Ogenki-desu-ka.* (How are you? —lit., Are you well?)
B: *Okagesama-de.* (Fine, thank you.)

and

A: *Oshigoto-wa doo-desu-ka.* (How's your work?)
B: *Okagesama-de.* (Thank you. It's going well.)

However, there always is the underlying idea that one should be grateful to what has been of help, even without one's knowledge. Even if one's success obviously comes from one's own effort, it is regarded as good to attribute it to others; this is why Mr. Okada said *Okagesama-de* to Mr. Lerner when he informed that his son has passed the entrance exam.

(March 13, 1977)

　　　おかげさまで、よくなりました

と答える。

　この場合は、相手が回復を助けたという意味ではない。自分の回復を可能にしたすべての要素に対し、その中には相手も含めて、感謝しているという気持ちを表しているのである。

　この「おかげさまで」はあいさつの形として固定して用いられることもある。

　　　A：お元気ですか（How are you? に当たる）
　　　B：おかげさまで（Fine, thank you. に当たる）

あるいは、

　　　A：お仕事はどうですか
　　　B：おかげさまで（Thank you. It's going well. に当たる）

などである。

　「おかげさまで」というあいさつの底には、自分が気づかずに恩恵を受けているものに対しても感謝すべきだ、という考えが流れている。自分の成功は明らかに自己の努力のたまものだと思われる時にも、人のおかげと言うことが高く評価される。隣家の主人が Mr. Lerner に息子の合格を告げる時に「おかげさまで」と言ったのは、このためである。

（1977.3.13）

Otsukaresama-deshita
おつかれさまでした
You must be tired

Last Saturday Mr. Lerner went shopping at a large supermarket downtown. There he took the elevator to the second floor. When the elevator started going upward, the girl at the door said

Shooshoo omachi-kudasai.
(Please wait a little bit.)

So he expected that he would have to wait a while, but the elevator reached the second floor in less than a minute. Then the girl bowed and said

Omatase-itashimashita.
(I'm sorry I kept you waiting.)

Mr. Lerner didn't think he had waited long enough to receive such a polite apology. He guessed that it was because the Japanese are always in a hurry and hate being kept waiting even for a short time. At the cashier's too, he was told that she was sorry to have kept him waiting a long time, although he had not waited more than two minutes.

Afterwards he went to the barber's near his house. When the haircut was finished, the barber said, while taking the white cloth off from around his neck,

Otsukaresama-deshita.
(lit., You must be tired.)

おつかれさまでした

You must be tired

　先週の土曜日、Mr. Lerner は商店街の大きなスーパーマーケットへ買い物に行った。店の中で、２階へ行くためのエレベーターに乗ったが、エレベーターがのぼり始めると、ドアのそばにいる女性が、

　　少々お待ちください

と言った。では、しばらく待たされるのかと思ったが、１分もしないうちに２階に着いた。若い女性はおじぎをしながら、

　　お待たせいたしました

と言った。
　こんな丁重な詫びを言ってもらうほど待ちはしなかった、と Mr. Lerner は思った。日本人はいつも急いでいて、ほんの少しでも待たされることを嫌うからだろうと彼は考えた。代金を払うレジでも、２分ぐらいしか待たなかったのに、お待たせしましたという詫びの言葉を聞いた。
　そのあと、近所の理髪店へ行った。調髪がすむと、理容師は首のまわりから白い布をはずしながら、

　　おつかれさまでした

と言った。
　やれやれ、Mr. Lerner のやったことと言えば、椅子にかけて、ぼんやりあれこ

Well, what Mr. Lerner had done was just sit in the chair and dream lazily about various things. He was not at all tired; he wanted to say that it was the barber himself that must have gotten tired. But before he could find the proper expression, the barber bowed and said

Shitsuree-itashimashita.
(lit., I'm sorry I was rude.)

*   *   *

Mr. Lerner felt that he had been treated very kindly all that day. When he met Sensee in the evening he said jokingly that he felt as if he had become a very old man, short-tempered and easily tired. Sensee laughed and said that was the way Japanese like to thank others. They often apologize or show sympathy to express their thanks. For instance, a train conductor often adds *Otsukaresama-deshita* to *Maido gojoosha arigatoo-gozaimasu* (Thank you for riding our train). Actually *Otsukaresama-deshita* means "Thank you for your patience" or "Thank you for your patronage."

Sensee gave another instance. A comedian may thank his audience by saying

Gotaikutsusama-deshita.

which literally means "You must be bored."

Mr. Lerner wondered if he should conclude his Japanese compositions with *Gotaikutsusama-deshita* or *Otsukaresama-deshita* or a combination of the two, to thank Sensee for the patience with which he corrected them. Sensee laughed and waved his hands to show rejection of this idea.

(April 2, 1978)

れ思いめぐらすことだけだった。全然つかれたおぼえはない。つかれたのは理容師自身ではないか、と彼は思った。しかし、それをうまく言う言葉を探しているうちに、理容師のほうにうやうやしく、

　　　失礼いたしました

と言われてしまった……。

＊　　　　　＊　　　　　＊

　Mr. Lerner は 1 日中、いたわられ通しであった。夕方先生に会ったので、冗談めかして、なんだか自分が、気短でつかれやすい大変な老人になってしまったような気がする、と言った。先生は笑って、それが日本式の感謝の表現なのだと言った。非礼を詫びたり、いたわりを示すことによって、感謝を表明するのはよくあることだと言う。たとえば、乗り物の車掌が「まいどご乗車ありがとうございます」のあとによく「おつかれさまでした」を加える。「おつかれさまでした」は、「ご辛抱くださってありがとうございます」「お引き立てありがとうございます」の意味なのだ。
　先生はもうひとつ、喜劇俳優が見物人に、

　　　ごたいくつさまでした

と言う例を加えた。
　Mr. Lerner は、自分も日本語の作文のしめくくりに「ごたいくつさまでした」か、「おつかれさまでした」か、あるいはその両方を、先生の忍耐強い添削の労に感謝するために書きそえるべきだろうかとたずねた。先生は笑いながら手を振ってその案を却下した。

（1978.4.2）

Oisogashii tokoro-o . . .
おいそがしい ところを…
When you're so busy . . .

Last Sunday afternoon Mr. Lerner visited Professor Takahashi to talk with him about the translation of his research. After an hour's discussion, the Takahashis asked him to have dinner with them. When he was leaving, he thanked Mrs. Takahashi for the meal and she thanked him for coming with a very polite expression starting with

Oisogashii tokoro-o . . .

(lit., The place where you are busy . . .)

Mr. Lerner didn't quite understand the use of the phrase *oisogashii tokoro-o.* It was Sunday and actually he didn't have much to do. Did Mrs. Takahashi say it just for formality's sake?

*   *   *

The phrase . . . *tokoro* refers to the situation; *yasunde-iru tokoro* means "while someone is taking a rest," and *oisogashii tokoro* means "while you're busy." The particle *o* is added to indicate the sense of "in spite of" or "regardless of." Thus *oisogashii tokoro-o wazawaza oide-kudasaimashite* means "you took the special trouble to come to see us although you're so busy." This phrase is used as a polite expression to greet a visitor whether personal or public.

In a public meeting, for instance, the master of ceremonies will usually

お忙しいところを…

When you're so busy . . .

　先週の日曜日の午後、Mr. Lerner は Professor Takahashi のもとをおとずれて、研究論文の翻訳について相談した。1時間ほど話し合ったあと、Takahashi 家の人たちに夕食をとっていくようにすすめられた。辞去する時、Mr. Lerner が Mrs. Takahashi に夕飯の礼を述べると、彼女は、

　　　お忙しいところを……

から始めて、極めて丁重に礼を述べた。

　Mr. Lerner は、「お忙しいところを」という表現をなぜ使ったのか、よくわからなかった。その日は日曜日で、実際のところ大した用はなかったのだ。あれは単なる儀礼であったのだろうか……。

＊　　　　　＊　　　　　＊

　「～ところ」は場面をさす。「休んでいるところ」は「休んでいる時」であり、「お忙しいところ」は「お忙しい時に」の意味である。助詞「を」を加えたのは、「～にもかかわらず」「～であるのに」の意味を表すためである。したがって「お忙しいところを、わざわざおいでくださいまして」は、「お忙しいのに特別の労をとって会いに来てくれた」の意味で、この表現は、個人的な場面でも公の場でも、来訪者を迎えるのに用いられる。

　たとえば大勢の集まりで、司会者は通常、

say something like

Honjitsu-wa oisogashii tokoro-o tasuu oatsumari-itadakimashite . . .
(I'm very happy that so many of you came to join us when you must be very busy.)

Not only the host uses this expression, but the visitor also often apologizes for taking the host's time, saying

Oisogashii tokoro-o ojama-shimashita.
(I'm sorry I took your time.)

(In this expression *tokoro-o* is used as the object of the verb *ojama-suru.*)

The underlying idea for this is that it is polite to presume that the listener must be busy and the speaker should feel guilty for causing him extra trouble.

In a similar way, one often says to someone who is going out

Odekake-no tokoro-o sumimasen-ga . . .
(I'm sorry to trouble you when you're going out, but . . .)

or

Oisogi-no tokoro-o . . .
(When you're in a hurry . . .)

Or, one often says to someone who has just finished work or returned from a trip

Otsukare-no tokoro-o . . .
(When you must be tired . . .)

(April 13, 1980)

　　本日はお忙しいところを多数お集まりくださいまして……

のようにあいさつする。主人側がこの表現を用いるだけでなく、来訪者も主人の
時間を費やしたことを詫びるために、よく

　　お忙しいところをおじゃましました

と言う。（この場合、「ところを」は「おじゃまする」という動詞の目的語として
用いられている。）
　こうした習慣の根底にあるのは、相手は忙しいに違いないと思うべきであり、
余計な労力をかけることを申し訳なく感じるのが礼儀である、という考えかたで
ある。
　同様に出かけようとする人には、

　　お出かけのところをすみませんが……

とか、

　　お急ぎのところを……

と言う。あるいは仕事を終えたばかりの人や着いたばかりの人には、

　　お疲れのところを……

という表現をよく用いる。

（1980.4.13）

Tasukarimashita
たすかりました
You helped me

Miss Yoshida was busy working all day yesterday, and it seemed she would be unable to finish her work by five o'clock. Mr. Lerner found some time to help her so that she could finish her work earlier. When the work was finished she thanked him and added

Hontoo-ni tasukarimashita.

(You really helped me.)

Mr. Lerner remembered that he had often wanted to say something nice when someone helped him and had wished he knew some expression other than *Arigatoo-gozaimashita.* He also remembered that once he had said

Tasukemashita.

to mean "You helped me," but it hadn't seemed to work.

*　　　*　　　*

The word *tasukaru* means "to be helped" while *tasukeru* means "to help someone." Saying *Tasukemashita* sounds as if the listener had helped someone other than the speaker. When one wants to thank someone for his help, one should use *Tasukarimashita* to mean "You helped me."

This expression can also be used when a third person has helped the speaker as in

助かりました

You helped me

　昨日 Miss Yoshida は一日中忙しく働いていたが、5 時までに仕事が終わらないようであった。Mr. Lerner は少し時間があったので手を貸して、仕事の終わりを早めるようにしてやった。仕事が終わった時、彼女は彼に礼を述べ、さらに、

　　ほんとうに助かりました

とつけ加えた。

　Mr. Lerner も、人が手伝ってくれた時は、「ありがとうございました」のほかに何かいいことを言いたいとよく思っていた。一度は "You helped me." の意味で、

　　助ケマシタ

と言ってみたこともあったが、それはまずかったようである……。

＊　　　　＊　　　　＊

　「助ける」は "to help someone" に当たり、「助かる」は "to be helped" の意味である。「助ケマシタ」と言うと、相手が話し手以外の人を助けたように聞こえる。自分を助けてくれたことに感謝するのなら、「助かりました」を使うべきである。

　「助かりました」は第三者が自分を助けてくれた場合にも、

Tomodachi-ga tetsudatte-kureta-node taihen tasukarimashita.
(My friend lent me a hand, so I was helped a great deal.)

Sometimes people feel that they are helped by nature. For instance when it has become pleasantly cool after serial hot days, they say

Kyoo-wa suzushikute tasukarimasu-ne.
(Today's nice and cool, so it helps us a great deal.)

When someone has thanked you for your help by saying *Tasukari-mashita*, you can either simply say *Iie*, or *Iie, doo-itashimashite* (You're welcome —lit., Far from it . . .). More politely you can say

Iie, taishita oyaku-ni tachimasen-de . . .
(No, I'm afraid I wasn't much help . . .)
Iie, nanno oyaku-nimo tachimasen-de . . .
(No, I'm afraid I wasn't any help . . .)

(June 15, 1980)

Nihongo-ga ojoozu-desu-ne
日本語が おじょうずですね
You speak Japanese very well

One thing recently bothering Mr. Ernest Lerner is that Japanese are too ready to praise his Japanese. When he says *Hajimemashite* instead of "How do yo do?" to introduce himself, they look surprised; when he says *Ii oten-*

　　　友達が手伝ってくれたので、たいへん助かりました

のように用いる。

　時には、自然が力を貸してくれたと感じることもある。たとえば暑い日が続いたあと快く涼しくなった場合、

　　　きょうは涼しくて助かりますね

と言う。

　「助かりました」と人が礼を述べた時には、簡単に「いいえ」あるいは「いいえ、どういたしまして」などと答える。もっと丁寧な言いかたとしては、

　　　いいえ、大したお役に立ちませんで……
　　　いいえ、何のお役にも立ちませんで……

のような表現がある。

（1980.6.15）

日本語がおじょうずですね

You speak Japanese very well

　この頃 Mr. Lerner が不愉快に思うのは、日本人がやたらに彼の日本語をほめそやすことである。紹介された時、"How do you do?" と言わずに「ハジメマシテ」と言うと、びっくりした顔をする。「イイオ天気デスネ」と言うと、「ラーナーさ

ki-desu-ne (It's a nice day), they say *Raanaa-san, nihongo-ga ojoozu-desu-ne* (You speak Japanese very well, Mr. Lerner). If someone is complimented on his English for just being able to say "How do you do?" and "It's a nice day," he would feel ridiculed. Being able to say two short sentences or phrases does not mean that one is good at the language.

Mr. Lerner sometimes suspects that Japanese regard foreigners as hopelessly poor at language learning.

*   *   *

It is easy and comfortable for anyone to talk with those who belong to the same group, but it requires some effort to speak to someone outside the group. This is especially true with people who sharply distinguish those "inside" from those "outside." Therefore most Japanese want to have certain exchanges before they can feel at home with a foreigner. These exchanges consist of certain questions and answers, or certain compliments and responses. Some typical questions are:

Okuni-wa dochira-desu-ka.
(Where are you from?)
Nihon-ryoori-wa taberaremasu-ka.
(Can you eat Japanese food?)
Nihon-wa nagai-desu-ka.
(Have you been in Japan a long time?)

And a typical compliment is

Nihongo-ga ojoozu-desu-ne.
(You speak Japanese very well.)

These questions and compliments are similar to "How do you do?" in

ん、日本語がおじょうずですね」と言う。もし英語で "How do you do?" とか "It's a nice day." と言っただけで、「英語がうまい」と言われたら、ばかにされたような気がするだろう。短い文や句が2つ3つ言えるからといって、その言語がうまいと言えるはずはないのだ。

日本人は、外国人には言語学習の能力が全くないものと思いこんでいるのではあるまいか……。

＊　　　　　　＊　　　　　　＊

だれでも、同じ集団に属している人間と話すのは、容易でもあり気楽でもあるが、集団外の人と話す時は、努力が必要になる。「ウチ」と「ソト」をきびしく区別する人々にとっては、なおさら努力が必要となる。したがって、大抵の日本人は一定のやりとりをしてからでないと、外国人と打ち解けて話す気になれない。そうしたやりとりには、ある程度の質問と答え、ほめ言葉とその反応などが含まれる。典型的な質問としては、

お国はどちらですか
日本料理は食べられますか
日本は長いですか

などがあり、典型的なほめ言葉としては、

日本語がおじょうずですね

がある。

こうした質問やほめ言葉は、相手から情報を得るためではなく、コミュニケーションのいとぐちを作るために用いられるという点で、英語の "How do you do?" などと似た性質を持つ。

日本人が必ずしもせんさく好き、おせじ好きということではない。質問したりほめたりすることは、往々にして、自分の集団から外へふみ出して外国人に接近

that they are used to confirm that the speaker and the listener are opening communications rather than to gain information.

The Japanese are not always being nosey or flattering; these questions and compliments are very often manifestations of their determination to step outside their own group and approach a foreigner, a step which requires a great deal of courage from most Japanese. The effort underlying this kind of exchange should be properly appreciated. This appreciation will help break up what many foreigners feel as a barrier between themselves and the Japanese.

(October 9, 1977)

Ee, maa, nantoka
ええ、まあ、なんとか
Well, somehow I manage

Mr. Lerner finds it difficult to respond to what Japanese say to him for the sake of politeness. A few days ago Mr. Saito praised his Japanese, so Mr. Lerner said as he had been told by Sensee

Iie, mada-mada-desu.
(No, I'm not any good at it yet. —lit., No, not yet.)

Then Mr. Saito admired this response so much that Mr. Lerner had to say something else, so he said

するという、大抵の日本人にとっては多大の勇気を要する行動に出る時の、決意を示すものなのである。この種のやりとりの底にある努力を、正当に評価しなければならない。その正しい評価が、多くの外国人が日本人との間に感じる壁を破るのに役立つであろう。

（1977.10.9）

ええ、まあ、なんとか

Well, somehow I manage

　Mr. Lerner は、日本人が礼儀上言ってくれることに対し、どう応対するかに苦労する。数日前にも、Mr. Saito が彼の日本語をほめてくれたので、先生に教えられた通り、

　　イイエ、マダマダデス

と答えたところ、その答えをまたほめるので、Mr. Lerner としてもまた何か言わねばならず、

Boku-nanka dame-desu-yo.
(I'm so poor at it. —lit., Such a person as me is no good.)

Mr. Saito still kept praising him so lavishly that Mr. Lerner said, in a desperate struggle to stop him,

Soo-desu-ka. Doomo arigatoo.
(Is that right? Thank you.)

This succeeded in stopping him, but Mr. Lerner felt that somehow he had done something wrong.

When he asked Mr. Takada about it, he said that he should have ended the topic quickly by saying

Ee, maa, nantoka.
(Well, somehow I manage.)

*   *   *

Japanese usually strongly deny any praise. (It is different between good friends.) But there are cases when it is difficult to simply deny someone's praise. For instance, when someone congratulates you on an achievement such as publishing a book or opening a store, it is not quite appropriate to say *iie*. There are ways of partially admitting the praise:

Ee, maa, nantoka.
(Well, I managed to do it somehow.)
Maa, okagesama-de nantoka.
(Thanks to everybody I could manage.)
Maa, koko-made-wa nantoka.
(I have managed so far.)

　　　ボクナンカ、ダメデスヨ

とやってみると、一段と大げさに感心する。ついにやけを起こした Mr. Lerner
が、もう止めてもらおうと、

　　　ソウデスカ、ドウモアリガトウ

と言ってやったら、目的は達成したが、やはりまずかったような気がした。
　Mr. Takada に聞いてみると、自分だったら、

　　　ええ、まあ、なんとか

と言って切りをつけただろう、ということであった……。

＊　　　　　＊　　　　　＊

　一般に日本人は人にほめられると強く否定する。（親しい友人の間では別であ
る。）しかし他人のほめ言葉を単に否定し去ることがむずかしい場合もある。た
とえば本を出版するとか店を開くというような業績をたたえられた場合、「いい
え」と答えるのは適切ではない。そのような場合の賛辞を部分的に認める方法が
ある。

　　　ええ、まあ、なんとか
　　　まあ、おかげさまでなんとか
　　　まあ、ここまではなんとか
　　　どうやらこうやら

などである。
　こうした表現は、目的の達成には苦労したし、達成はしたが、決して満足すべ
き成果はあがっていない、ということを示す。

Dooyara kooyara.

(Somehow or other.)

These expressions show that you have achieved something with much difficulty and that the achievement is not at all satisfactory.

If you feel it is too hypocritical to deny completely your acquaintance's praise about your Japanese, you can say

Okagesama-de nantoka sukoshi-wa wakaru-yoo-ni natte-kimashita.

(Thanks to you, I am beginning to understand a little bit.)

(October 23, 1977)

　日本語が上達したという賛辞を完全に否定し去るのは、あまりにも偽善的であると感じる場合には、

　おかげさまで、なんとか少しはわかるようになってきました

のように言うことができよう。

（1977.10.23）